"A spice journey for everything a home cook nee[ds]
Indian food, through authentic family recipes."

In *New Indian Basics*, Preena Chauhan and Arvinda Chauhan—the masters behind Arvinda's Indian spice blends—present a collection of flavorful, accessible recipes and kitchen wisdom gained from a lifetime of personal and professional experience teaching Indian cooking, where spices take center stage. With their clear instructions and signature warmth, this mother-daughter duo will guide you to flawless renditions of Indian dishes, both traditional and modern, with absolute ease.

Here, you'll find recipes perfect for all meals and all home cooks, whatever the time of day or level of experience. Chapters like Indian Brunch & Eggs are full of modern dishes like Chai-Spiced Apple Buckwheat Pancakes with Maple Cream or Indian-Style Baked Eggs in a richly spiced tomato sauce. Indian Street Foods & Savory Appetizers will make traditional snacks, like Chaat Papri, your new go-to nibble. And whether you're looking for vegetarian or meat mains, you'll find options to excite your palate, from a classic Butter Chicken or Channa Masala to a celebratory Vegetable Biryani with Saffron & Nuts or a Mapled Tandoori Salmon with Mint. There are many accompaniments that go along with a full Indian meal, so there are chapters dedicated to these components such as chutneys, pickles, raitas, and masalas to help you build your pantry, rice dishes, and, of course, flatbreads, like homemade Naan. And don't forget about dessert! Preena and Arvinda share a full chapter on exquisite mithai, traditional sweets, and modern desserts as well. With this focus on the many expansive regions that make up India's culinary fabric, you'll be enticed to learn about beloved specialties and new flavor profiles. No matter the recipe, Preena and Arvinda use their many years as educators to walk you through every step.

In addition to their vibrant recipes, Preena and Arvinda include helpful resources like a spice glossary, a guide to different lentils and beans, a mini workshop on the best way to cook basmati rice, and information on how to serve—and eat—an Indian meal. They even suggest ways to put it all together with their celebratory and seasonal Indian menus. With a wealth of incredible recipes, knowledge, and gorgeous photography, *New Indian Basics* is sure to become a food bible in your kitchen.

PREENA CHAUHAN
& ARVINDA CHAUHAN

Co-founders of Arvinda's Indian Spice Blends and Cooking Classes

NEW INDIAN BASICS

100 Traditional and
Modern Recipes from
Arvinda's Family Kitchen

appetite

Appetite by Random House® and colophon are registered trademarks of Penguin Random House LLC.

Library and Archives of Canada Cataloguing in Publication is available upon request.

ISBN: 9780525611318
eBook ISBN: 9780525611325

Cover and book design by Andrew Roberts
Photography by Reena Newman, with photos on pages iii, 10, 18, 28, 129, 209, 255, 272 by Sandy Nicholson
Printed in China

Published in Canada by Appetite by Random House®,
a division of Penguin Random House LLC.
www.penguinrandomhouse.ca

10 9 8 7 6 5 4 3 2 1

Penguin
Random House
Canada

This cookbook is
dedicated to our elders
and ancestors, who
have guided us through
writing this book.
Thank you for passing
on your knowledge,
immense wisdom, and
culinary traditions
down the generations.

TABLE OF CONTENTS

INTRODUCTION

My first foray into the kitchen was at around the age of five. I would help my mother, Arvinda, sort out beans and lentils and do odd jobs for her in the kitchen. I loved to bake and made my first cake at this age—incidentally, this was about the same age as my mother when she first started cooking. Although we have that in common, our circumstances couldn't be more different.

When Arvinda was seven years old, living with her family in a small village in Kenya, her mother passed away, so she started cooking out of necessity from a young age, helping her grandparents while her father was away studying in Germany and the U.K. Her first cooking experience was making chapatis on a chulha, a traditional earthen or clay stove heated by fire, which is a cooking method still used today. To care for her four siblings, she learned to grind fresh flour through a heavy grinding stone and pound spices using a large mortar and pestle. What started out as an obligation early on in her childhood later turned into her lifelong passion, as cooking and food became a channel for my mother to express her creative passions.

My parents moved to Canada in the early 1970s, and my mother's love of cooking continued to grow. Over the years, she developed her skills as an Indian cook, learning to create curries according to traditional family recipes. She gradually understood the intricacies and nuances of spices, using this knowledge to cook delicious curries and dals that quickly became family favorites. She churned out complete Indian meals—savory appetizers with delicious chutneys, traditional Indian flatbreads prepared fresh and piping hot, fragrant jeweled basmati rice, and, of course, delectable Indian sweets for dessert. My mother experimented with international and Indian recipes and treated us to delicious home-cooked meals every single day.

During a Canada Day celebration in Hamilton, Ontario, in 1993 while we were volunteering for a fundraising initiative for a women's charity, we sold a variety of Indian snack foods like pakoras and dal wadas (lentil fritters) to help raise money. After receiving numerous inquiries about how to make these savory Indian treats at home, I recall my mother offering ad hoc cooking instruction on the spot, enthusiastically explaining how to make these tasty appetizers with only a few simple ingredients. The adventurous people kept asking if there was somewhere they could go to learn this. It was at that very moment that my mother discovered how much she loved to teach people how to cook Indian food, so she began setting up a business to start teaching Indian cooking classes that coming fall.

Since the very start of her cooking classes, my mother wanted to demonstrate how to prepare healthy Indian meals at home with easy cooking methods using simple ingredients and fresh spices. She called her cooking classes Healthy Gourmet Indian Cooking, and her approach was always uncomplicated. She taught about spices and how they could be used to cook curries of depth with bold, layered, and delicious flavors. She also added a gourmet flair to traditional Indian foods, presenting them a little differently, more elaborately or upscale. Cooking-class participants delved deeply into spices, the cornerstone of traditional Indian cooking. In her eight-week Indian Beginner's Cooking course, participants learned about the storied history of spices, how spices are grown and cultivated, how they are used and stored in an Indian kitchen, and, most notably, that quality spices and ingredients are essential for the best-tasting Indian foods. During these classes in the early 1990s, I assisted my mother in her cooking school every step of the way (most of the classes were held on weeknights and weekends at various locations across the Greater Toronto Area), taking in all the cooking knowledge along with the students, who were also eager to learn.

My mother and I travelled to the exotic spice-growing regions of India and Sri Lanka to see and learn firsthand how spices are cultivated, harvested, and brought to market, meeting passionate farmers, traders, and spice merchants along the way. In the mid- to late-2000s, we took our students to India through guided culinary tours. Around this time, our students, noticing the freshness and quality of spices being used in our classes, often asked to purchase these spices directly from us. They also sought advice on how to make Indian cooking even easier, which prompted my mother to mix together a few key spices into a batch of masala (meaning "spice blend") for her students to try. She started stocking premixed roasted and ground garam masala and chai masala at the request of her students. The masalas became so popular among the students that they requested that we bring them to market.

During this time, I was pursuing my Master in Environmental Studies at York University and received a small amount of funds to start a small business. Inspired by the Food Network's show *Recipe for Success*, which profiles entrepreneurs who were successful in bringing a family recipe to market, my brother Paresh and I launched Arvinda's Indian spice blends. With a slight amount of savings in hand, we started grinding small-batch spice blends in a modest industrial unit in Oakville, Ontario, that we had converted into a food-production facility. We started marketing Arvinda's masalas at trade shows in Toronto and won over the likes of celebrity chefs, who asked to buy food-service sizes for their acclaimed restaurants in Toronto—an exciting development for us right at the launch of the brand.

In 2005, when the company started, most customers and people in the grocery industry didn't even know what a masala was, often mistaking the word *masala* for marsala, the famous Sicilian wine, and making it difficult to gain traction in the market early on. Over the next decade, Paresh and I worked tirelessly to introduce Arvinda's

blends to customers and educate grocery buyers on how to make healthy and easy curries from scratch using spices at countless cooking demonstrations, cooking classes, farmers' markets, trade and consumer shows, and culinary events across Ontario and in Montreal, Quebec.

Now, with nearly 30 years of teaching others Indian cuisine and learning our craft of spice roasting, grinding, and blending through Arvinda's Indian spice blends, we share with you all our Indian cooking traditions, knowledge, tips, and techniques in *New Indian Basics*.

Just as in our cooking classes, our goal is to encourage, inspire, excite, and empower you to venture into the fascinating cuisine of India so you can create your favorite Indian foods or try some brand-new recipes with delicious results for yourself and your family. Many of the recipes in this cookbook are some of our most-loved family recipes taught in our cooking classes, while others are inspired by our travels. There are recipes for all occasions and for everyday Indian meals. Some are rustic and home-style, while others are extravagant, to be enjoyed during the festival time of year and the holidays. There's a little something for every Indian food lover in this cookbook.

Spices are healing. Spices are powerful. Spices tell a rich story. And spices taste incredible and are what make Indian food so delicious. In this cookbook, we pay homage to Indian spices, using them throughout and encouraging you to embrace them for their mouthwatering flavors, good health, and bold taste.

Cook with spice, happy life!

Preena

Preena

SPICES & INGREDIENTS GLOSSARY

Listed below are spices, ingredients, and terms commonly used in this cookbook, grouped by category:

Aromatic Whole Spices

BLACK CARDAMOM

Larger than green cardamom pods and dark brown in color, black cardamom lends a smoky and mild eucalyptus-like flavor to savory Indian dishes such as biryani. Use sparingly, and always remember that black cardamom is not a substitute for green!

BLACK PEPPERCORNS

Native to India and grown on the Malabar Coast, black peppercorns are derived from small dried berry-like fruits and are widely used whole and ground in Indian cooking to lend peppery heat and flavor. Black peppercorns are referred to as black gold and the king of spices.

CINNAMON

Native to Sri Lanka, true cinnamon comes from the fragrant inner bark of the *Cinnamomum verum* tree and has a rich, sweet flavor. For Indian curries, we favor the outside cinnamon bark, and use pieces roughly 2½ inches long. It's thicker and coarser and has an intense, spicy flavor. The bark is added to meat dishes, sweet chutneys, and rice dishes. For the best results, use cinnamon bark from India, found at South Asian grocery stores.

CLOVES

The dried flower buds of the tropical myrtle tree and grown in India for over a century, cloves are usually used whole in curries and rice dishes and may be fried, roasted, or ground according to the recipe. Clove is a key ingredient in garam masala and chai masala and works wonders for a toothache and a sore throat due to its medicinal value of acting as a mild anesthetic.

GREEN CARDAMOM PODS

Affectionately known as the queen of spices and native to South India, green cardamom contains tiny black, fragrant seeds and is known for its sweet, perfumy fragrance, while the larger black cardamom is known for its smoky flavor. Note that the two are not interchangeable. Cardamom pods are used whole in curries and rice dishes, and the ground spice is an important aromatic in garam masala, chai masala, and Indian sweets.

MACE

Beautiful orangey-yellow, mace is the lacey dried outer casing of the nutmeg seed and has a milder nutmeg flavor and similar warming aroma. In this book, mace is always used in a dried whole form in curries and ground into masalas.

NUTMEG

An important spice in chai masala and garam masala, nutmeg has a distinct, sweet flavor and a beautiful heady aroma ideal for Indian sweets. Purchase nutmeg whole and grate as needed.

SAFFRON

One of the world's most expensive spices, saffron comes from the orangey-red stigmas of the crocus flower. In India, saffron is grown in Kashmir and is used sparingly in festive dishes such as biryanis, meat curries, sweets, desserts, and drinks. Choose a premium pure saffron for the best color and flavor.

STAR ANISE

The dried seed pod of an evergreen shrub native to East Asia, each star anise can contain up to eight seeds. It lends a distinct licorice flavor to curries when cooked whole and is an ingredient in garam masala.

WHITE PEPPERCORNS

White peppercorns are derived from the same berries of the black peppercorn, but when picked are soaked to remove the outer skin. The result is a mellower but more earthy and pungent flavor perfect for Perfumy Chai Masala (page 46).

Coconut

COCONUT

A key ingredient in South Indian cuisine, coconut is used in all its forms, including fresh, dried, and desiccated. Coconut oil and milk are both used to make curry sauces.

Dairy Products

DAHI

Dahi refers to homemade Indian-style yogurt (see Creamy Dahi, page 40).

PANEER

A neutral-flavored pressed Indian cheese made from cow's milk, paneer does not melt when cooked, retaining its shape when simmered in a curry or when grilled. Make it from scratch using the Homemade Fresh Paneer recipe (page 154).

RAITA

Raita is a cooling yogurt condiment delicately spiced with cumin seeds and/or mustard seeds and containing grated cucumber and sometimes cubed tomatoes. It is served with appetizers, curries, rice, and flatbreads. See Basic Cooling Cucumber Raita (page 60).

Fat

GHEE

Ghee, or clarified butter, is regular butter with the milk solids and salts removed. The benefit of using ghee is that it doesn't burn like butter when you cook at high temperatures, and it lends a distinctive rich and nutty taste to curries, dals (lentil curries), rice pullaos, and desserts. Try making Homemade Ghee (page 39).

Flavorful Seeds

AJWAIN SEEDS

Strongly flavored, bitter, and pungent with an earthy quality, ajwain seeds are tiny, grayish-brown, and used in Indian vegetarian dishes, snacks, and flatbreads. They're also known as bishop's weed or carom seeds. Use them sparingly, as a little goes a long way!

CARDAMOM SEEDS

Within the pod of a cardamom lies tiny black seeds containing all the cardamom flavor. These seeds can be finely ground into a powder or coarsely ground. In this book, recipes calling for cardamom seeds (or cardamom powder) always use the seeds of green cardamom pods (not black cardamom pods!) either coarsely ground or finely ground.

CORIANDER SEEDS

See cilantro/coriander (page 8).

CUMIN SEEDS

Used either whole or ground into a powder, cumin is one of the most frequently used spices in Indian cuisine. Whole seeds are roasted and ground for use in raitas, salads, and chutneys. In the powdered form, cumin is one of the foundational spices in a curry. Cumin also aids in digestion.

FENUGREEK

An annual plant, fenugreek is cultivated in vast quantities in India, where the seeds, fresh leaves, and dried leaves (see kasoori methi, page 8) are all used in cooking. The yellow seeds of the fenugreek plant are highly aromatic, bitter, strongly flavored with an aroma reminiscent of maple syrup, and commonly used in Indian pickles. Fresh fenugreek leaves, known as methi, are used in flatbreads, Indian snacks, meat curries, and vegetable dishes.

FENNEL SEEDS

Small greenish seeds with a licorice-like flavor, fennel seeds are used in masalas such as Panch Phoran (page 49). Commonly served at the end of an Indian meal, fennel acts as a digestive aid and is a natural breath freshener.

MUSTARD SEEDS

Brown mustard seeds are an important spice in South Indian, Bengali, and vegetarian cooking. When placed in hot oil, mustard seeds pop and release an intense flavor.

NIGELLA SEEDS

Known as kalonji, these tiny black seeds impart a fantastic toasted-oniony flavor to a curry and are a main ingredient in Panch Phoran (page 49).

Flours

BESAN
See chickpea flour, below.

CHAPATI FLOUR
Also known as atta, this is a very fine, soft whole wheat flour used in many Indian flatbreads, including chapatis, paranthas, naan, and deep-fried puris.

CHICKPEA FLOUR
Gluten-free! Also known as gram flour or besan, in Indian cooking this flour is always made from channa dal. It is used mostly as a thickener in curry sauces and in batters for Indian snacks, fried appetizers, flatbreads, and sweets, and can be purchased from South Asian grocery stores.

SUJI
The Hindi word for semolina, also known as rava or cream of wheat, suji is derived from wheat and is available coarse or fine. Suji is a main ingredient in puris, as in Suji Puris (page 205) and the popular Indian sweet Warm Suji Halwa (page 249).

Ground & Pungent Spices

AMCHOOR
Derived from unripened green mangoes that are dried and ground into a fine powder, amchoor imparts a sour and tangy taste to Indian foods. This is a main ingredient in Tangy Chaat Masala (page 48).

ASAFOETIDA
Known as hing, this spice is a dried plant resin that has a pungent odor and a bitter taste, so it is usually used only in pinches! It is often used in bean and lentil dishes to impart a unique flavor and to aid in digestion.

CHILI POWDER
The fruit of the capsicum plant and native to tropical America, chilies were introduced to India by the Portuguese. Always use a 100% pure chili powder from India, which provides the heat level, color, and flavor necessary for Indian cuisine. Purchase from South Asian grocery stores or from a reputable Indian brand. A key ingredient in Indian cuisine, chili powder adds heat to a dish, so add as little or as much as you like, according to your taste.

Dried chilies

CILANTRO/CORIANDER

Seeds of the cilantro plant, known as coriander seeds, are used whole or ground into a powder, adding a mellow and lemony flavor to Indian dishes. It is a foundational spice in a curry: choose Indian coriander powder, which will provide the correct flavor profile for Indian cooking. The fresh cilantro leaf (also known as Chinese parsley or coriander leaf) is a common herb used as a garnish and to make sauces and chutneys.

DRIED RED CHILIES

Sometimes known as Kashmiri dried red chilies, these whole red chilies are used mainly for presentation and don't lend the same level of heat as chili powder. Purchase dried red chilies from a South Asian grocery store.

KASHMIRI CHILI POWDER

Also known as Kashmiri mirch, this chili powder imparts a milder chili heat and flavor to Indian dishes than the aforementioned chili powder, while providing a natural bright red color. This is a great substitute for chili powder for those who enjoy milder flavors. Do keep in mind, however, that it still does lend some heat!

TURMERIC

A member of the ginger family and a bright golden color, turmeric is available as a fresh root or in a powder form. Turmeric powder is widely used in Indian cooking and gives a curry its unique yellow color. Use in small quantities to avoid bitterness. One of India's most beloved spices, turmeric is known to be a "super spice" with an abundance of medicinal value, such as aiding in digestion, acting as a powerful antioxidant, and possessing anti-inflammatory and anti-bacterial qualities, to name a few.

Indian Herbs, Fresh & Dried

CILANTRO

See coriander/cilantro (page 8).

CURRY LEAVES

An important ingredient in South Indian cooking, this dark green leaf has a distinctive, bright aroma, imparting a beautiful and unique mild citrus-like flavor. With an intense aroma, the flavor pairs well with potato, vegetable, and lentil dishes as well as with coconut-based curries. Curry leaves are a signature and key flavoring ingredient in Goan Pork Vindaloo (page 171). Fresh is best! If fresh is not available, good-quality dried curry leaves will suffice.

KASOORI METHI

The name for dried fenugreek leaves, kasoori methi has a savory, herby aroma with celery- and fennel-like notes, and act as a powerful flavor enhancer in curries toward the end of the cooking process to add boldness and depth to the dish. Rub the kasoori methi between your fingers before adding them into the dish to release their full flavor.

Lentils & Beans

DAL

Lentils or beans that are either whole, split, and/or hulled are known as dal. *Dal* also refers to a cooked dish of lentils in the form of a curry or a lentil soup.

KEY LENTILS & BEANS

See Cooking with Lentils & Beans, page 19.

PAPADS

Gluten-free! These thin, crispy lentil wafers are fried or toasted, and served with a vegetarian thali or any full Indian meal. See Cumin-Scented Papads (page 211).

Rice

BASMATI

An aromatic rice variety of delicate fine grains, basmati is India's most revered rice and the key ingredient in pullaos and biryanis. Try to find a premium quality of basmati rice for optimum results, as grades may vary. Higher-quality varieties are usually more expensive.

Preena stirring jaggery

PATNA

A long-grain rice grown in the Patna Plains in East India's state of Bihar, Patna rice can be used in some recipes such as Basic Boiled Fluffy Rice (page 214). Milder in flavor with denser grains than basmati, patna rice serves well with saucy and spicier curries.

PULLAO

A delicately spiced rice dish with ghee and spices such as cumin, cardamom, saffron, or other aromatic spices.

Salt

BLACK SALT

Also known as kala namak or Himalayan black salt, black salt is a rock salt containing sulfurous compounds. Its bold, pungent flavor—reminiscent of hard-boiled eggs—can be balanced when combined with other spices. With a unique flavor all its own, black salt is a key ingredient in Tangy Chaat Masala (page 48).

Souring Agent

TAMARIND

Commonly referred to as the Indian date, tamarind is one of the primary souring agents in Indian cuisine. Tamarind is widely used in meat, poultry, and dal dishes and is the key ingredient in the popular Sweet & Tangy Tamarind Date Chutney (page 54). Tamarind comes in a block form or a concentrated paste sold in a small plastic jar. For the recipes in this book, we recommend the paste for its ease of use and intense flavor. Store it in the refrigerator to extend its shelf life to over a year.

Sweet

JAGGERY

An unrefined sugar derived from sugarcane, jaggery is available in the form of a block or a paste. It is used as a wholesome sweetening agent reminiscent of brown sugar, with molasses-like and caramel notes. Jaggery, also known as gur, imparts a unique flavor to curries and Indian sweets. Anytime we want to add a sweet taste to a curry, we always use jaggery if it's available. A good substitute is maple sugar.

COOKING WITH INDIAN SPICES: THE BASICS

You'll never find an Indian cook without their prized masala dabba, a round stainless-steel box that houses at least seven different spices and is exceedingly airtight to protect their flavor and freshness. Throughout human civilization, spices have always been treated with this kind of reverence. Centuries ago, some spices were worth more than gold—black peppercorns native to the Malabar Coast in South India were referred to as black gold, as weight to weight they were priced higher than the precious metal!

Today in Indian homes, spices are still highly cherished and greatly valued. Any diligent cook takes great care in purchasing, storing, and using the best quality of these culinary gems because spices are what Indian cuisine is all about! I grew up appreciating the value of spices, and from our many visits to spice plantations, I learned how painstakingly laborious the process of cultivating spices can be.

Because spices are so important to an Indian cook, we want to share some important points to consider when selecting spices for Indian cuisine. Having worked with spices in both Indian cooking and in manufacturing Arvinda's masalas, we know that these nuances can make all the difference to the end results.

1 | NOT ALL SPICES ARE CREATED EQUAL

When shopping for spices, consider the quality factor. In spice auctions, spices are sold in different tiers or grades. For example, cardamom pods come in different sizes; the jumbo pods contain more seeds and are more fragrant, so are more favorable for sweet dishes and desserts, whereas the smaller pods are ideal for cooking. Spices should be a vibrant color—an indication of freshness—and should not appear dull or muted. Spices should look alive and smell fragrant, and when you are cooking with good-quality spices, your kitchen should fill up with their heady aromas. Of course, the best indicator of quality is the flavor in your finished dish.

2 | ORIGIN

Here we would like to emphasize the importance of choosing spices of Indian origin for Indian cooking, as this allows the flavors to be true to an authentic taste. For example, a Mexican chili powder shouldn't be substituted for Indian chili powder, as it will lend a different flavor profile altogether—perhaps adding a smokiness that may not be found in Indian chilies. Spices from India have a particular flavor based on their terroir—the soil, geography, and climate where they are cultivated. When all the spices are sourced with this particular flavor profile, the dish will taste distinctively Indian.

3 | STORAGE TIPS FOR FRESHNESS

When purchasing spices, it is important to choose the freshest source and then store them properly so they retain freshness. A stainless-steel masala dabba (see page 27) is handy and the most practical way to store the vast array of Indian spices for a number of reasons. First, because stainless steel is inert, it will not react with the spices to change their flavor in any way or reduce their quality. Second, the airtight outer lid minimizes the air flow into the box, which helps preserve aromas and flavors longer, and an inner lid seals each individual spice container on the inside. Finally, the opaque stainless-steel box blocks out light, which can degrade spices. Spices are sensitive to light, so if you're storing your spices in glass jars, be sure to tuck them into a cupboard or drawer so they're not exposed to direct sunlight or fluorescent light. Because heat also affects the quality of spices, store your masala box in a cooler part of your kitchen, away from an oven or an appliance that generates heat.

4 | GENERAL SHELF LIFE OF SPICES

Purchase all your individual whole and ground spices in small quantities and use them fully before replenishing. Once the spices lose their flavor and aroma, they are of little use and will not lend much taste to your cooking, so use them within one year of purchasing. It is a good practice to label your spices with the purchase date to help you remember when to discard them. The general shelf life for highly aromatic blends such as chai masala and garam masala spices is nine months to one year. For more pungent spice blends such as panch phoran, chaat masala, or other masalas using cumin, turmeric, and chilies, the expected shelf life can be up to 15 months.

The recipes in New Indian Basics can be also made with Arvinda's signature masalas. Visit arvindas.com for a masala conversion guide.

THE MAGIC OF MASALA

Spices are what make Indian cuisine so mouthwatering, intoxicating, and addictive, bringing sheer pleasure to both spice lovers and Indian food lovers alike. In the "Cooking with Indian Spices" section (page 11), we discussed how important it is to be discerning when selecting each individual spice for Indian cooking, as collectively they deliver a sizable amount of the flavor in your Indian dishes.

Now we turn the discussion to masalas, which is where all the magic in an Indian kitchen *really* starts to happen! As an artist, my mother often analogizes cooking Indian cuisine to painting a picture. Both are creative endeavors to bring a vast number of individual elements together in a work of art. In a recipe, the main ingredients—such as paneer, chicken, or dal—are very similar to the artist's clean canvas, begging to be sprinkled with flavors, salted and seasoned, and nuanced with hints of pungency, sourness, or heat. Spices act as the paint on a painter's palette—a diversity of flavors and aromas at your fingertips to create your masterpiece of a curry exactly the way you want to enjoy it. What's fun about Indian cooking is that as you're tasting, simmering, adding more spices and more flavor, then tasting again, there comes a precise moment when you've hit the perfect flavor combination for you, a gratifying instant when you have balanced out the curry just right!

What Is a Masala?

Masala is a generic word used in South Asia to describe any mixture or combination of spices. It can be a simple mixture of just a couple of spices, or a more complex blend of up to a dozen or more. Whether you're using just a few spices or many, the challenge when creating a masala from scratch is achieving the correct balance, which is one of the complexities of Indian cooking. When cooked, an unbalanced spice blend may taste as if something is missing or overpowering. When I was first learning to cook Indian curries from my mother, she would taste my dish and know exactly what it was lacking. Sometimes it was only a pinch of salt, and other times she would add a heaping ½ teaspoon of coriander powder, but either way, a masala needs the spices to be balanced to perfection.

Arvinda Chauhan's 1973 painting. As an artist, my mom views Indian cooking as an art form.

COOKING WITH LENTILS & BEANS

Lentils and beans are the primary source of protein for India's hundreds of millions of vegetarians, and they are used so extensively in Indian cuisine, it is little wonder that the two are virtually synonymous. In India, the custom of eating a vegetarian diet relying on lentil and bean plant-based sources of protein dates back at least 2,500 years, and is rooted in the tradition of Ayurveda, India's ancient natural system of medicine.

The variety of ways in which lentils and beans are used in the Indian kitchen is astounding and a testament to the ingenuity and creativity of India's culinary history. Whether lentils and beans are used whole or split in dals and curries or ground into a fine flour to prepare mouthwatering snacks, appetizers, and indulgent desserts, their beauty is their versatility and how well they take on the flavors of spices.

When my mother began teaching Indian cooking classes in the 1990s, she dedicated a session of her eight-week Indian Beginner's Cooking course solely to lentils and beans. Class participants often had misconceptions about cooking and eating lentils, such as that they're difficult or time-consuming to prepare, that they shouldn't ever be cooked in a pressure cooker, and that, when eaten, they induce gas in the digestive system. Our students would sometimes panic at the mere sight of the pressure cooker! My mother would show its safety mechanisms, the proper way to seal it, and how much water to add. Despite this, there was still a lot of apprehension about using the kitchen appliance we had been using in our home for as long as I can remember.

A lot of the misconceptions we heard about 25 years ago have changed or disappeared altogether now that more and more people have embraced plant-based diets and are eating and cooking with more lentils and beans. New vegetarians and people who are seeking plant-based options naturally turn to Indian cuisine for the immense variety of vegetarian meals and foods made with pulses, and because they're spiced so deliciously. More appliances have come onto the market as aids to safely cook dried lentils and beans at home, one of them being the Instant Pot.

I take much pride in sharing our lentil and bean recipes, as they make up a huge part of my Indian diet and are a mainstay in my repertoire of weekly recipes. I love lentils even more for the fact that they're grown in abundance right here at home, on the Canadian prairies.

Here are our top tips for cooking with lentils and beans:

---

1 | **Purchase in small quantities:** Purchase dried lentils and beans as required and in small quantities. This way, you'll always go through your stocks quickly and they won't have a chance to get old. We recommend using dried lentils and beans within one year of purchase; if they are older than that, the cooked result will be tough or rubbery.

2 | **Rinse well:** Always rinse dried lentils and beans in several changes of warm water to lift off any dirt on the surface. This will also release excess starch, which shows up as bubbles in the water during the cleaning process.

3 | **Soak before cooking:** When boiling or using a pressure cooker to cook lentils and beans—especially the larger varieties—it's important to soak them in advance to reduce the cooking time and ensure they cook well from the inside out; doing so also helps make them more digestible.

4 | **Remove scum or dirt after cooking:** After cooking lentils or beans, be sure to remove or discard any scum or dirt present on the top or the side of the pot or pressure cooker before proceeding to cook the recipe.

5 | **Use enough water and salt:** If using a pressure cooker, always fill it with enough water to cover the lentils or beans, and sprinkle in the salt (usually about 1 teaspoon for the recipes in this cookbook).

Rajma

Urad (Whole)

Moong Beans (Whole and Sprouted)

Toor Dal

Urad Dal
(Split)

Urad Dal
(Split and Hulled)

6 | Choose the right lentil or bean:

Choosing the correct lentil or bean for a recipe can be confusing, as a recipe may call for moong beans, split moong dal, or split and hulled moong dal—so, what is the difference? In Indian cuisine, lentils and beans are used in all their various forms for different applications. Here is a depiction of the various lentils and beans used in this cookbook in their different forms. When shopping for lentils and beans, look for these names to purchase the correct type:

BLACK-EYED PEAS
Black-Eyed Peas (Whole)

KABULI CHANNA
Channa (Whole Chickpeas)

KALA CHANNA
Kala Channa (Whole Indian Chickpeas)
Channa Dal (Indian Chickpeas, Split and Hulled)

MASOOR
Masoor (Whole Red Lentils)
Masoor Dal (Red Lentils Hulled)
Masoor Dal (Split and Hulled Red Lentils)

MOONG
Moong Beans (Whole and Sprouted)
Moong Beans (Whole)
Moong Dal (Split)
Moong Dal (Split and Hulled)

RAJMA
Rajma (Whole Red Kidney Beans)

TOOR
Toor Dal (Split and Hulled Pigeon Peas)

URAD
Urad (Whole Black Lentils)
Urad Dal (Split Black Lentils)
Urad Dal (Split and Hulled Black Lentils)

Masoor (Whole)

Kala
Channa

Masoor
Dal
(Hulled)

Channa
Dal

Black-Eyed Peas (Whole)

Moong Beans
(Whole)

Moong Dal
(Split)

Masoor Dal
(Split and Hulled)

Moong Dal
(Split and Hulled)

Kabuli Channa

CURRIES, CURRIES & MORE CURRIES!

Virtually synonymous with Indian cuisine, the term *curry* conjures up images of various orangey-reddish hues of tomato gravies with morsels of meat or seafood, or turmeric-colored lentil and bean preparations, steaming hot and wafting heavenly aromas. When speaking of Indian foods, even those unfamiliar with Indian cuisine would think of a curry first—it being the dish that has become India's culinary trademark. But the term in English is oversimplified. Historical influences, a vast geography, a range of available ingredients, strong regional uniqueness, and foods sensitive to culture and religion have influenced and shaped the foods coming from the Indian subcontinent. In India, these dishes are referred to by their proper names, as in dum aloo, korma, vindaloo, saag paneer, and so on, rather than labelled with the catch-all term *curry*, which is common outside of India. With each dish bearing distinct flavors, it isn't really fair to say a curry is just one dish with the same spicing, which is why you'll notice we refer to all the dishes in this cookbook by their proper names rather than by *curry*.

That said, in this cookbook, we tend to use three typical bases for our eventual curries:

ONION & TOMATO BASE

This is the most popular base for a curry, where the onions are caramelized and the tomatoes, whether fresh or in a concentrated crushed form, make up the base of the curry sauce. The majority of the dishes in this cookbook use the onion and tomatoes combination. An example of this curry base is Shahi Paneer (page 159).

TOMATO BASE

In some curries, onions are absent and the tomato makes up the sauce. In this case, an intricate spice balance is required to make the dish flavorful, and the result is more of a reddish curry sauce. Examples of this base are Kashmiri Dum Aloo (page 137) and Pantry Channa Masala (page 121).

ONION BASE

With the absence of tomatoes, the onions are the star of the show and take on more flavor, and the result is a yellower curry. An example of this curry base is Lamb Korma (page 184).

Below are the tips we share in our Curries, Curries & More Curries cooking class to create flavorful and delicious curries at home:

OIL

There are some specific recipes where you should use homemade ghee and virgin coconut oil, but for all other recipes, choose a high-quality oil that is neutral in flavor and has a high smoking point, such as avocado oil, sunflower oil, or grapeseed oil.

CHOPPING THE ONION

The size of the cut onion for the curry is important, which is why our recipes call for finely chopped onions. If you have trouble chopping the onion fine, use a food processor or mandoline. When you take a bite of a curry, very rarely will you take a bite of a big piece of onion, which can be off-putting. Most of the time, the onion makes up the sauce but you don't even notice.

CARAMELIZING THE ONION

One of the most important steps in making a curry from scratch is to caramelize the onion so that the sweetness is fully brought out and the onion becomes golden brown. We recommend you do this in a high-quality non-stick pan with a wider base, and cook on medium-low heat if you have the luxury of time. Most of our recipes ask you to do this step on medium-high heat but with continuous stirring, so the onions do not burn.

COOKING RICE, THE INDIAN WAY: A MINI WORKSHOP

One of the most sought-after rice varieties is basmati rice, and rightfully so. Treasured in India and desired around the world for its unique heavenly aroma and beautiful fine long grains, basmati rice is cultivated in the North Indian states of Haryana, Punjab, Himachal Pradesh, Uttarakhand, Uttar Pradesh, Jammu, and Kashmir, making India the top producer of basmati rice, accounting for over 70% of the world's production.

Apart from basmati rice, other rice varieties are also heavily consumed in Indian cuisine, namely Patna rice, a long-grain variety that is primarily cultivated in the Patna Plains of the state of Bihar. For those recipes that call for long-grain rice, try to use this variety.

One of my favorite foods to cook is a basmati rice pullao, and I love teaching others how to get perfect results every single time. My interest in the Indian style of rice making was sparked when I was in my teens, when I soaked up my mother's rice-making methods and tips. I recall my mother telling her students that a lot of pressure is on the cook to present a perfect, beautiful rice dish to family and guests. An Indian rice should never be oversalty, mushy, undercooked, or overcooked—if it is any of these things, all the accompanying curries get ruined in one broad swipe! Even if everything else is presented perfectly, the Indian dining experience is compromised without perfectly prepared rice, and with all the hard work that goes into making an Indian meal, it's a shame for it to be judged on a single dish!

Here are our foolproof steps and tips for the perfect basmati rice pullao:

1 | Place 1 cup of basmati rice in a large bowl. At the sink, rinse the rice in several changes of lukewarm water—not hot and not cold! I know it's tempting, but avoid using your hands to massage the rice, as this will break the grains and result in mushy rice. Fill the bowl with water and dump out the starchy cloudy water; repeat until the water runs relatively clear.

2 | Fill the bowl with fresh lukewarm water and allow it to soak for 10 minutes. It's important not to exceed 10 minutes or the result will be mushy rice. Set a timer if you think you may forget!

3 | Drain the rice completely.

4 | In a wider-based pan (not a pot), melt 1 teaspoon of ghee and add ½ teaspoon of cumin seeds. Add the drained rice and, using a flat utensil, gently fold the rice grains so each grain is coated with the ghee. Sprinkle in 1 teaspoon of salt.

5 | Add about 1½ cups water. I usually don't measure the water but just add enough to cover all the grains of rice. Put the lid on and bring to a boil on medium-high heat; cook until all the water is absorbed.

6 | At this stage, check if the rice grains are cooked by pinching a couple of grains with your index finger and thumb. If it is still al dente, sprinkle in a little water and put the lid back on and either cook for a couple of minutes or allow it to sit for 5 to 10 minutes off the heat. The steam itself can sometimes finish off the cooking process.

7 | Fluff the rice with a fork before serving and always garnish with a luxurious sprinkle of garam masala and cilantro. Serve the rice piping hot in the pan so it remains hot when enjoying it with your favorite curries!

THE INDIAN KITCHEN

Cooking authentic Indian meals at home requires some basic utensils, listed below. In most Indian kitchens, pots, storage containers, utensils, and plates are traditionally made from stainless steel, which is favored for its non-reactive properties.

BELAN: A thin rolling pin typically made of wood and tapered at each end, allowing you to form chapatis and other Indian flatbreads into perfect circles. A substitute for a belan is a thicker tapered rolling pin.

BLENDER: Used to make fine and smooth chutneys and pastes.

FOOD PROCESSOR: Indispensable for processing main ingredients such as onions, garlic, and ginger.

GHEE CONTAINER: A small stainless-steel container to store prepared ghee.

KADHAI: An Indian-style wok for deep-frying, stir-frying, and sautéing. It can be made out of stainless steel or iron.

KATORI: A small stainless-steel bowl with straight edges to present food on a thali (see photo).

MANDOLINE: A kitchen utensil with a variety of attachments used to efficiently and uniformly slice or julienne vegetables.

MASALA DABBA (OR MASALA BOX): A round container that typically stores about seven different spices. Masala boxes come in various sizes (small, medium, and large). Stainless steel is an excellent choice, and an airtight lid helps to extend the shelf life of spices. A filled masala box should be stored in a cool, dark place.

MORTAR & PESTLE: Used to grind spices, nuts, or other ingredients into a finer grind. Available in various materials such as stone, marble, wood, granite, or brass, and comes in various sizes (small, medium, and large). We recommend a medium-sized stone mortar and pestle, which is ideal for finer spice grinding.

NON-STICK POTS & PANS: Non-stick pots are especially recommended for dry curries or any recipe that calls for caramelizing onions, and a wider non-stick pan is recommended for rice pullaos. Choose high-quality non-stick pots and pans.

PARAAT: A shallow stainless-steel dish with high edges used for making Indian flatbread dough the traditional way.

PRESSURE COOKER: A good-quality stainless-steel pressure cooker is essential in an Indian kitchen to efficiently cook lentils and beans in only 10 to 15 minutes, depending on the lentil or bean. Always follow the user manual to ensure you exercise safety at all times.

SEV MAKER: Also known as a sevai maker, this is a traditional stainless-steel or brass utensil that acts as a press with a hand crank to make various snacks, including sev. It comes with various disks with different-sized holes to make various snack shapes.

STAINLESS-STEEL POTS & PANS: Heavy-bottomed stainless-steel pots and pans are recommended for cooking curries.

STAND-UP MIXER: Using the dough hook, this is a handy appliance for easily mixing flatbread doughs together.

TAWA: A griddle made of cast-iron used for cooking Indian flatbreads at a high temperature. A good-quality frying pan or skillet is a good substitute.

THALI: A stainless-steel plate housing a number of smaller stainless-steel bowls to serve a full Indian meal.

Masala Dabba and other utensils used in the Indian kitchen

HOW TO SERVE AN INDIAN MEAL

Very rarely does one eat an Indian curry on its own. For example, you would never sit down with just a bowl of channa masala, because if served all on its own, the dish would be too bold and intense. However, when channa masala is paired with a flatbread and boiled rice, with pickles and raita on the side, the dynamic of the meal changes dramatically; the flavors of the curry become balanced, mellower, and extremely enjoyable. Therefore, when planning to cook an Indian recipe, it is important to consider what other items you will serve along with it. For themed and special-occasion menus, we offer a number of suggestions in the Festive & Seasonal Indian Menus on page 267, but for everyday Indian meals, the guidelines below will help you assemble an Indian meal quite easily.

All over the Indian subcontinent, curries, rice, flatbreads, and different types of condiments are eaten, but each region has its own specialties and combinations. How the meal is assembled and served, however, is generally the same throughout.

An Indian meal in its simplest and most traditional form is served on a thali, a stainless-steel dish or plate that holds small stainless-steel bowls (called katoris). Both the thali and the small katoris are straight-edged. This is common Indian dinnerware. In Kerala, the traditional meal or feast would be served on a banana leaf, known as a sadhya.

Not only is the plate itself called a thali, but the meal is also referred to as a thali, with the most common being a vegetarian thali. One of our most memorable meals ever was in a New Delhi canteen, where we ordered an Andhra thali, meaning it was a plateful of specialties hailing from the southeastern state of Andhra Pradesh. About 16 different items were placed on the thali, including a spicy mango pickle; a deep-fried,

doughnut-like, savory fritter; spicy dals; vegetable curries; boiled rice; curd; and sweets.

Similarly, when you travel throughout India and visit roadside restaurants or truck stops, known as dhabbas, located on the major thoroughfares or at canteens or restaurants, you can order many different regional thalis, such as a Rajasthani thali, Punjabi thali, Gujarati thali, and so on. A thali as a meal can contain just a few items or a dozen or more, such as the elaborate Andhra thali we experienced and always remember so fondly.

The simplest thali from any region of India may contain the following items:

- One or two dals
- One or two vegetable curries
- A flatbread
- A rice dish
- A savory appetizer like a pakora or bhajia
- A mithai (an Indian sweet)
- Papads or pappadums
- Dahi (homemade yogurt) or raita
- Chutney or condiments
- Achar (pickles)
- Lassi or a buttermilk beverage
- Cucumber or a raw cut vegetable of some sort
- Drinking water, served at room temperature

When consuming these together, all the senses get fired up: touch, sight, smell, taste, and even sound come into the fold, especially if sitting in a bustling dhabba where the activity level is high and servers come around offering second helpings of curries, rice, flatbreads, or water! The thali lends the eater infinite flavor combinations, which creates excitement, pleasure, and adventure with every single bite!

HOW TO EAT AN INDIAN MEAL

Toward the end of our cooking classes, when everyone had been served their meal and we were about to dive into a heaping plate of curry, some would be ready with fork and knife in hand! We had to take a moment to guide the group on the correct way to eat an Indian meal—which is with the hand. To be exact, you use your dominant hand to break off a piece of flatbread, scoop up some of the curry, and dip it into some pickles or a chutney. You also eat rice with the same hand, using your fingers to scoop up a handful of rice and place it in your mouth.

It's understandable if you're not used to eating a meal with your hand—it can definitely feel a little unnatural at first. But after only a few tries, you'll find that the food tastes all the more delicious. There are several reasons for this, the main one being that when you eat with your hand, you gain a deeper connection to the experience of eating itself. You can feel every morsel of food with each fingertip, adding the sense of touch to the eating experience, along with smell, taste, and sight. The senses become fully engaged.

Eating with your hand also allows you to take smaller, fewer bites, as you can take only what you're able to grasp within the fingers. This allows you to be more mindful and to take the time to sit and enjoy the meal. You may even find you become satiated more quickly. The act of eating with your hand is a full sensory experience, allowing you to be present in the moment and making the act of eating a spiritual connection to the self.

Finally, when eating with your hand, not one morsel of food ever gets wasted.

The next time you sit down to enjoy an Indian meal, inhale deeply, charge your senses, and dig in with your hand!

Breaking off a piece of a flatbread.

Dipping the flatbread into a curry.

Scooping up a handful of rice.

ESSENTIAL TIPS FOR INDIAN COOKING

Below is a short list of tips that will help make your Indian cooking quick and efficient.

PREPARE ONIONS & HERBS IN ADVANCE

If you know you'll be doing a fair bit of Indian cooking during the week, peel a few onions in advance and store them in an airtight container in the refrigerator. The same goes for cilantro, which we use in almost every recipe. We recommend rinsing and draining the whole bunch, trimming the roots off, patting it dry, and storing it in an airtight container in the refrigerator for up to a few days. When even these small steps are done in advance, it makes the meal preparation easier.

PREPARE GARLIC & GINGER PASTES IN ADVANCE

This is one of Arvinda's favorite time savers! Garlic and ginger pastes are much easier to make in a large batch than in small quantities for individual recipes. We recommend making it in a food processor—for garlic paste, add 1 to 2 cups peeled garlic cloves and process until fine and smooth. Press the paste into a pie plate and cover it with plastic wrap. Do the same for chopped peeled gingerroot. As soon as the garlic paste and ginger paste freeze, cut them into cubes (or use an ice-cube tray to freeze the paste to begin with). Transfer the frozen cubes of garlic and ginger to separate airtight containers and return them to the freezer. This will prevent the strong aromas, especially of garlic, from transferring to the other foods stored in your freezer.

USE TIME-SAVING APPLIANCES

To cut down the cooking times in the recipes, use a good-quality pressure cooker or Instant Pot for cooking lentils and beans, a food processor for finely chopping onions, and a stand-up mixer with the dough hook for preparing flatbread dough. These appliances help us to make a full Indian meal every single day quickly with ease. Always refer to instruction manuals for safety and usage guidelines before use.

KEEP TWO SETS OF MEASURING SPOONS HANDY

It's handy to dedicate one set of measuring spoons to wet ingredients and one to dry ingredients, namely the spices, so you don't have to keep washing and drying a single set.

MAKE CHOPPING EASY

A dedicated pair of kitchen shears or scissors for cooking comes in handy when you need to finely chop green chilies or herbs such as cilantro or mint. While I personally love chopping vegetables manually with a cutting board and my favorite knife, my mother prefers to use a mandoline or a food processor to help with quick chopping. We use a lot of onions in Indian cooking, and a good-quality mandoline can work wonders with finely chopping them—important when creating a delicious curry from scratch. As with all kitchen tools and appliances, take precautions and read the user manual for safe operation.

MAKE CURRIES ONE DAY IN ADVANCE OF SERVING

When making an Indian meal, consider making the curries one day in advance of serving. The spices will continue to release their flavor and the curries will take on depth and become much more delicious. If the curry includes meat, it will marinate in the spices. Making the curries in advance also frees you up to make the appetizers, flatbreads, and rice on the day of serving so they are fresh.

MEASURE INGREDIENTS IN ADVANCE

We recommend *mise en place*—the French phrase used to describe having all ingredients ready, chopped, and measured before you start cooking. This is very important in Indian cooking, as once you start doing a tarka or vaghaar (tempering of the spices in hot oil or ghee on medium-high heat), the spices can burn quickly. If you're chopping in between steps or rushing to get your ingredients ready, this may compromise your results. You can do *mise en place* for spices as well, especially if you're pulling them from different containers, rather than a masala box. This will help you add all the spices to the dish accurately and precisely.

GRIND SPICES IN STAGES

If using a clean coffee grinder for grinding masalas, first do a coarse grind in a mortar and pestle to break down larger spice pieces, such as whole nutmeg and cinnamon sticks. You can then proceed with a finer grind in the coffee grinder.

USE A MASALA DABBA

Having all your spices conveniently on hand in a single container saves a lot of time and allows you to add them to the dish with ease. We typically use three masala dabbas: one containing ground and pungent spices, such as cumin powder, coriander powder, chili powder, turmeric powder, cumin seeds, and brown mustard seeds; a second for housing our aromatic whole spices, including cardamom pods, cinnamon sticks, whole cloves, and peppercorns; and a final box for different types of sea salts, jaggery, sesame seeds, and other pantry items used in Indian cooking. It's important to keep like spices together in one masala box so their aromas do not interfere with one another. As an artist, Arvinda sees the masala box similar to how a painter prizes their palette. The spices are the colors of creativity, and you can get inspired to create something delicious the moment you open your masala box.

1

MAKING HOMEMADE DAIRY PRODUCTS

With an immense population of dairy cows, India is the world's largest producer of milk, making dairy ubiquitous in Indian cooking for its flavor, as a source of protein, and for its nutritional benefits. Making milk products such as ghee and dahi at home is a common practice, so when a recipe calls for them, one always has them readily on hand. Homemade versions are fresh and delicious and are well worth the effort!

HOMEMADE GHEE

As olive oil is to Italian cooking, ghee is to Indian cooking, so we can't even begin to cook Indian cuisine without a discussion about ghee. Deliciously golden with a warm and toasted buttery aroma, ghee is simply clarified butter, meaning that the milk residues, solids, and salts are removed from the butter to create a pure form of fat. While not essential to every Indian dish, ghee is very important to every Indian meal. Ghee is mostly used in dals, pullaos, biryanis, some curries, flatbreads, and desserts. Even as little as a teaspoon can completely transform a dish, adding beautiful nutty, buttery flavor to every bite.

PREP TIME: 1 MINUTE

COOK TIME: 45 MINUTES

YIELD: ABOUT 1 CUP

½ pound unsalted butter

1 | In a small non-stick, heavy-bottomed saucepan on low heat, melt the butter. Do not stir. Allow the butter to come to a very gentle simmer, continuing to cook until a transparent liquid forms at the top and milk residues settle at the bottom of the pan.

2 | Once the liquid is golden and the milk residue at the bottom is slightly brown, the ghee is ready. This can take anywhere from 30 to 45 minutes.

3 | Remove from the heat. Using a fine stainless-steel strainer, immediately strain into a heatproof jar or stainless-steel ghee container.

NOTE: Discard any milk residues, as they can't be used in cooking. To extend the shelf life of ghee, store it in the refrigerator and it will keep for up to 1 month.

CREAMY DAHI

I clearly remember that, when I was little, I'd come into the kitchen after dinnertime and see the oven light still on. Inside the oven was a stainless-steel pot containing my mother's dahi (dahi is the Hindi word for homemade Indian-style yogurt)—also commonly referred to as curd in India. After the evening meal, she often took advantage of the warm oven to make a batch of homemade yogurt, particularly in the winter months when it wasn't humid enough to let the yogurt set on the counter. In Indian homes, making homemade yogurt is very common, as it is ubiquitous in the Indian diet. Yogurt is indispensable for cooling the palate to counter the spiciness of curries, as a digestive aid, and for adding protein to vegetarian diets. We use it in condiments such as raita, to thicken up a curry sauce, or in a dessert such as Decadent Shrikhand (page 234).

PREP TIME: 20 MINUTES, PLUS 4 HOURS (OR MORE) SETTING

COOK TIME: 10 MINUTES

YIELD: 4 CUPS

5⅓ cups whole milk
⅓ cup Balkan-style yogurt

1 | Preheat the oven to 250°F, then turn the oven off.

2 | In a medium heavy-bottomed pot, bring the milk to just under a boil (when small bubbles start to form on the surface). Do not stir. At this point, immediately remove the pot from the heat and set aside to cool to lukewarm temperature, about 15 to 20 minutes.

3 | Whisk in the yogurt until it becomes frothy.

4 | Transfer the mixture to a medium stainless-steel bowl or oven-safe dish and place it in the center of the warm oven for at least 4 hours or until the dahi sets. Once the dahi has set, refrigerate immediately.

NOTE: In the summer, if your kitchen temperature is higher than 78.8°F, leave the bowl on your kitchen counter overnight to allow the yogurt to set, rather than using the oven.

2 | MAKING MASALAS AT HOME

Simply said, without spices there is no Indian cooking!
Their freshness and balance can make or break a curry, and this
is where the art of masala making comes in. A masala, the Hindi
word for "mixture of spices," can be a combination of any number
of individual spices. When making masalas at home, choose
top-quality spices and make them in small batches, tweaking
the formulation to your liking. In this chapter, we create five
versatile masalas to be used with the recipes in this cookbook.

Perfumy Chai Masala
(page 46)

Panch Poran
(page 49)

Warming Garam Masala

Tandoori Marinade
Spice Blend
(page 47)

Tangy Chaat Masala
(page 48)

WARMING GARAM MASALA

The rajah of Indian spice blends, garam masala is the quintessential Indian cooking ingredient. For an Indian cook, garam masala is always close at hand—a delicate pinch for a garnish, a light dusting for a seasoning, or a slightly heavier amount when cooking an aromatic curry. Generally made from five to a dozen different whole spices, garam masala can either be sweet, hot, aromatic, savory, or anything in between, and it varies from region to region and family to family. Proudly passed from one generation to the next, a family's garam masala recipe is a time-honored treasure and the defining centerpiece of their style of Indian cooking. Our beloved garam masala recipe is aromatic and sweet, with the use of fragrant spices such as cardamom, nutmeg, and cinnamon. We mainly use it as a beautiful garnish on curries, rice dishes, and biryanis.

PREP TIME: 15 MINUTES

COOK TIME: 5 MINUTES

YIELD: ¾ CUP

1½ tablespoons fennel seeds

1½ tablespoons green cardamom pods

2 teaspoons black peppercorns

2 teaspoons whole cloves

1½ teaspoons cumin seeds

1 teaspoon coriander seeds

1 teaspoon whole mace pieces

9 bay leaves

5 star anise

4 cinnamon sticks

1 whole nutmeg

1 | Heat a small skillet to medium-high and add all the spices. Using a wooden spoon, gently stir the spices until they become slightly golden brown and fragrant. You can also hold the handle of the skillet to gently toss the spices until they become toasted. This may take a couple of minutes, but the real indicator is when the cumin seeds are light golden and the cardamom pods slightly swell.

2 | Remove the spices from the heat. Once they cool, place them in a medium or large heavy mortar and pestle and grind into a fine powder. Alternatively, grind the spices in a clean coffee grinder on the finest setting.

3 | Store the garam masala in a stainless-steel container or an airtight jar and keep it in a cool, dark place. For optimal flavor, use within 9 to 12 months.

NOTE: Warning! Take care not to toast the spices at a very high temperature, as they can quickly burn. If you find that medium-high heat is too high, reduce the heat to medium. A heavy-bottomed skillet will also help prevent the spices from burning.

PERFUMY CHAI MASALA

My great-grandfather was a chai connoisseur, as was my grandfather, who needed his morning masala chai. Having a chai ritual to start the day seems to run in the family, and I too inherited this tendency, adding my own panache and even opening up a masala chai cafe called Arvinda's Spices & Chai with my brother, Paresh. I've seen my mother carve out time for masala chai every single day as far back as I remember—she always seemed to have a steamy cup of homemade masala chai close by! After school, the kitchen was often heavy with the perfumed aromas of freshly cracked cardamom, nutmeg, cinnamon, and cloves, which meant another fresh batch of chai masala had just been roasted and ground.

PREP TIME: 15 MINUTES

COOK TIME: 5 MINUTES

YIELD: ½ CUP

WHOLE SPICES

2 tablespoons green cardamom pods

1 teaspoon fennel seeds

1 teaspoon whole cloves

1 teaspoon whole mace pieces

½ teaspoon black peppercorns

½ teaspoon white peppercorns

4 cinnamon sticks

1 whole nutmeg

GROUND SPICE

1½ tablespoons ginger powder

1 | TOAST THE WHOLE SPICES: Heat a small skillet to medium-high and add all the whole spices. Using a wooden spoon, gently stir the spices until they become slightly golden brown and fragrant. You can also hold the handle of the skillet to gently toss the spices until they become toasted. This may take a couple of minutes, but the real indicator is when the cardamom pods slightly swell.

2 | Remove the whole spices from the heat. Once they cool, place them in a medium or large heavy mortar and pestle and grind into a fine powder. Alternatively, grind the spices in a clean coffee grinder on the finest setting.

3 | BLEND THE GROUND SPICE: Stir in the ginger powder until the chai masala is uniform.

4 | Store the chai masala in a stainless-steel container or an airtight jar and keep it in a cool, dark place. For optimal flavor, use within 9 months.

TANDOORI MARINADE SPICE BLEND

The word tandoori *must have you thinking* about the well-loved North Indian grilled specialty, tandoori chicken, but let's think about changing that! In its most authentic form, a tandoori spice blend is mixed with yogurt, lemon juice, garlic, and ginger to create a marinade for this popular succulent grilled dish, but the same blend also creatively doubles as a versatile and flavorful seasoning. This savory, heady blend works beautifully when rubbed onto root vegetables or to season hearty chickpeas, like in our Tandoori-Spiced Chickpea Salad (page 70) or Indian-Spiced Deviled Eggs (page 74).

PREP TIME: 10 MINUTES

YIELD: ½ CUP

2 tablespoons sweet paprika

1½ tablespoons coriander powder

1 tablespoon Warming Garam Masala (page 45)

1 tablespoon Kashmiri chili powder

2 teaspoons Indian chili powder

2 teaspoons cumin powder

1 teaspoon amchoor

1 | In a large mortar and pestle or medium bowl, place all the ingredients and mix until the spice blend is uniform.

2 | Store the tandoori marinade spice blend in a stainless-steel container or an airtight jar for up to 12 months, keeping it in a cool, dark place.

3

CHUTNEYS, PICKLES, RAITA & SALADS

Alongside any Indian meal you will find a selection of fresh chutneys, raitas, pickles, and fresh salads, which add layers of flavor to an already flavor-intense meal. Chutneys add freshness, sweetness, and heat, while raita cools the palate to counter spiciness. Pickles add sour and hot, while Indian salads are simple and cooling and cleanse the palate between bites of different dishes. The recipes in this chapter are brilliantly versatile and can be used over and over to round out your Indian meals, elevating them to a whole other level.

Minty Green Cilantro Chutney

Sweet & Tangy
Tamarind Date
Chutney (page 54)

Hot Chili Tomato Chutney (page 55)

MINTY GREEN CILANTRO CHUTNEY

If you're planning to prepare only one chutney for an Indian meal, let it be this one. The liveliest of Indian chutneys, ours is packed with refreshing mint and, when combined with cilantro, brings green yummy freshness to any Indian meal. Balanced with heat from green chilies and the flavors of warm cumin, the result is a chutney so versatile it can be paired with virtually any Indian food, but it goes best with savory snacks and appetizers, often in tandem with other chutneys, like Sweet & Tangy Tamarind Date Chutney (page 54). Add more chilies to ramp up the heat or omit them altogether as per your taste.

PREP TIME: 15 MINUTES

YIELD: 1 CUP

1½ cups fresh mint leaves, stemmed

1 cup coarsely chopped fresh cilantro

¼ cup water

1 small Gala apple, peeled and finely cubed

½ medium tomato, cubed

2 cloves garlic

2 small green chilies, stemmed, or to taste

1 teaspoon cumin seeds

1 teaspoon freshly squeezed lemon juice

¾ teaspoon sea salt, or to taste

1 | In a blender, combine all the ingredients and blend into a smooth paste. Serve this chutney fresh and store it in an airtight jar in the refrigerator for up to 4 days.

NOTE: You can make this recipe in a bigger batch, but be careful about increasing the green chilies and salt—both can be added to taste. Any leftovers can be refrigerated for up to 4 days or frozen for a couple of months. If freezing it, when ready to serve, thaw out the chutney and mix it into some dahi or yogurt for a quick condiment on the side!

SWEET & TANGY TAMARIND DATE CHUTNEY

Sweet, sour, and dark brown, this chutney is the essential tangy condiment for either dipping into or drizzling on top of Indian snacks and appetizers. Part and parcel with samosas, India's most celebrated snack food, this chutney is also served with Indian street-food favorites such as Savory Chaat Papri (page 91) and Masala Makai (page 97), a savory corn appetizer. Premade versions of this chutney often contain a lot of refined sugar and have a syrupy consistency. This recipe uses the natural sweetness of dates to balance out the sourness of the tamarind, and no sugar is added, which I absolutely love. In our cooking classes, I'm always excited to share this recipe, not only because it's a healthier option, but also because I know a pleasing and delicious Indian savory snack food is on the menu and will soon follow!

PREP TIME: 10 MINUTES, PLUS 4 HOURS SOAKING

YIELD: ¾ CUP

1 cup pitted dates

¾ cup hot water

1 tablespoon concentrated tamarind paste

½ teaspoon Warming Garam Masala (page 45)

½ teaspoon sea salt, or to taste

¼ teaspoon Tangy Chaat Masala (page 48)

Pinch of Indian chili powder

1 | In a small bowl, rinse the pitted dates in a couple of changes of warm water. Drain and cover with the hot water and soak for 4 hours (or overnight). This allows the dates to soften so they can be blitzed into a smooth paste.

2 | In a blender, add the dates, including the soaking liquid, and the rest of the ingredients. Blend until smooth. You may need to add a little extra water to achieve the desired consistency.

3 | Transfer to a small bowl and serve with Indian appetizers. Store in an airtight glass jar or container in the refrigerator for up to 1 week.

HOT CHILI TOMATO CHUTNEY

This delicious chili-spiked tomato chutney *is our answer to when you're feeling inclined to reach for a bottle of ketchup. As children, my brother and I liked to dip our pakoras in ketchup for sweetness to help offset the spiciness, while the adults savored theirs with a fresh chutney, such as Minty Green Cilantro Chutney (page 53). This chutney is like a hybrid of the two—tomatoey and sweet and loaded with fresh cilantro and mint. This chutney pairs particularly well with Tandoori-Spiced Fish Pakoras (page 105) or Mom's Favorite Garam Masala Omelet (page 78).*

PREP TIME: 10 MINUTES

YIELD: ABOUT 1¼ CUPS

½ cup unsalted crushed tomatoes

1 large ripe tomato, cubed

½ cup coarsely chopped fresh cilantro

½ cup coarsely chopped fresh mint

2 tablespoons water

1 teaspoon sweet paprika

½ teaspoon sea salt, or to taste

½ teaspoon garlic paste

½ teaspoon jaggery or raw cane sugar

1 to 2 small green chilies, stemmed and chopped, or to taste

1 | In a blender, add all ingredients and blend until smooth. You may need to add a little extra water to achieve the desired consistency. Store this chutney in an airtight glass jar or container in the refrigerator for up to 3 days.

NOTE: Fresh green chilies are vibrant, lending a clean hit of heat necessary for a chutney. When adding chilies to a chutney, it's best to add one at a time, tasting the heat level as you go—add more if you desire more heat and stop when you've reached your limit. If you've gone too far with the chilies, you can correct the flavor by adding extra tomato and perhaps even a small apple to add more volume and sweetness to the chutney and offset any undesired heat.

SOUTH INDIAN FRESH COCONUT CHUTNEY

During our trips to South India, mornings would start in the most idyllic way—an early morning yoga class in a lush tropical setting, followed by a savory South Indian breakfast of uttapams served with an array of fresh chutneys, freshly pressed fruit juices, and cut local exotic fruits, all enjoyed in the hot morning sun. After breakfast, we would walk to the local market to procure ingredients needed for the day's cooking. In South India, this means a fresh coconut or two! The market vendor would swiftly cut the coconut open upon request, first releasing the coconut water, then cracking the hard exterior with a cleaver, presenting it in pieces to take back with us. The process to prepare fresh coconut at home is just the same, although I open it with a hammer similar to how I watched my father do it when I was growing up. Once opened, the fresh coconut is finely grated or minced and ready to be cooked into curries and chutneys such as this one.

Being a cooked chutney, the preparation of this one differs from that of others. Fresh curry leaves and mustard seeds are tempered in hot coconut oil, then the finely grated or minced coconut is gently cooked for only a few minutes, retaining its textured crunch. Although this chutney is best suited for a South Indian meal, I also find myself adding a spoonful to a simple dal or a dollop on top of a vegetable curry—which instantly reminds me of walking alongside coconut-tree-lined paths on the way to the market, taking me back to those sultry and blissful Kerala days!

PREP TIME: 20 MINUTES

COOK TIME: 10 MINUTES

YIELD: ABOUT 1½ CUPS

1 small fresh coconut or 1 cup dried desiccated coconut, unsweetened

1 tablespoon coconut oil

¼ teaspoon brown mustard seeds

3 dried red chilies

1 green chili, sliced lengthwise

8 to 10 fresh curry leaves

½ cup water

¼ cup Creamy Dahi (page 40) or Balkan-style yogurt

½ teaspoon sea salt, or to taste

1 | To crack the coconut if you're using a fresh one, the first step is to use a corkscrew to open the three germination holes, also referred to as the eyes of the coconut. Once it's open, strain the coconut water into a cup or bowl and reserve it for another use.

2 | Place the coconut on a cutting board. With a hammer, strike it firmly along the middle equator, rotating it so its exterior is cracked all the way around. Where it is cracked, pry the coconut open using a utensil or your hands (see Note for an alternative method).

3 | Insert a small paring knife between the exterior shell and the flesh to remove the flesh for cooking. Any brown skin attached to the flesh can be removed with a vegetable peeler.

4 | In a food processor, process the fresh coconut flesh until finely minced. Measure 1 cup minced coconut and reserve any extra for a South Indian–style curry.

(continued)

5 | In a small non-stick pot on medium-high heat, heat the coconut oil. Add the mustard seeds and fry them for 30 seconds or until they begin to pop. Add the dried red chilies and green chilies and mix, frying for a few seconds. Add the curry leaves and fry for 15 to 30 seconds or until they glisten in the oil.

6 | Add the coconut, water, dahi, and salt. Mix and cook on medium heat for at least 5 minutes, taking care not to boil the chutney. Fresh coconut may release more moisture than dried desiccated coconut, so you may have to cook the chutney for a few more minutes if using fresh, until the moisture is absorbed.

7 | Serve this savory chutney with any South Indian meal.

NOTE: Fresh whole coconuts are available in South Asian grocery stores and large grocery retailers. Once you've opened the germination holes in step 1, an alternative method for opening the coconut is to place it in the palm of your hand and, using the blunt side of a large knife (or cleaver), strike the coconut around the middle equator, rotating it so you can crack it all the way around. Once cracked, pry it open to get access to the flesh. Remember safety precautions and take extra care if you're using this method. If fresh coconut is not available, simply substitute it with high-quality unsweetened dried desiccated coconut for an easier method and comparable results!

MATCHSTICK CARROT & GREEN CHILIES ACHAR

India has a deep-rooted tradition of pickling, with each family having their favorites—from tart mango, to chili lime pickles, to sour cherry, to endless more varieties written in the family cookbook! An Indian meal is at its best when at least one fiery, soury, spice-infused pickle is within reach. Pickles add pungency and extra layers of flavor to the Indian meal, making each and every bite that much tastier. Indian-style pickles pair perfectly with vegetarian curries and dals and are a must-have on any vegetarian thali or with an Indian-style brunch.

PREP TIME: 20 MINUTES

YIELD: ABOUT 1 CUP

1 medium carrot, peeled
8 small green chilies
2 teaspoons brown mustard seeds
1 teaspoon fenugreek seeds
1 teaspoon sea salt
½ cup sunflower oil
3 tablespoons mustard oil

1 | Cut the carrot into 2-inch long matchsticks (or julienne). Rinse the green chilies and pat to dry. Slice the green chiles lengthwise, leaving on the stems. Set aside.

2 | Using a medium or large heavy mortar and pestle or a clean coffee grinder, grind the mustard seeds and fenugreek seeds until coarsely ground. A grind between fine and coarse (not too fine like a powder and not too coarse that the seeds are merely broken) is perfect for achar! If grinding the spices manually in the mortar and pestle, keep in mind that the fenugreek seeds are harder to break down using this method and may require a bit of extra arm work.

3 | In a medium jar (one that holds 2 cups or slightly less), place the carrots and the green chilies vertically. Sprinkle the ground mustard and fenugreek seeds, and the salt, evenly on top. Carefully pour the sunflower oil on top, then add the mustard oil. Put the lid on and gently swirl the jar so the achar ingredients combine.

4 | Store these pickles in the refrigerator and consume fresh within 3 to 4 days of preparation.

NOTE: If you don't have mustard oil on hand, just use the ½ cup sunflower oil on its own. The results will be just as delicious!

BASIC COOLING CUCUMBER RAITA

Raita is an Indian yogurt-based condiment that's light, creamy, and cooling and commonly contains refreshing cucumber. It goes well with a wide range of Indian meals, working its magic when met with hot and spicy foods. While there are many variations to a raita recipe, our suggestion is to keep a light hand with the seasoning and the spicing because the Indian meal itself will already be bold in flavor. In Ayurveda, the cooling properties of cucumber are known to pacify heat (or agni) generated in the body from spicy food and hydrate the palate during the meal, while the yogurt also plays an active role in neutralizing spiciness. If you unexpectedly bite into a fiery green chili, it is a spoonful of our trusted raita, more than a glass of water, that comes to the rescue to douse the heat!

PREP TIME: 20 MINUTES

YIELD: ABOUT 1½ CUPS

½ English cucumber

½ teaspoon brown mustard seeds

½ teaspoon cumin seeds

1 cup Balkan-style yogurt

¼ teaspoon sea salt

½ teaspoon garlic paste

Pinch of Kashmiri chili powder, to garnish

Fresh cilantro, finely chopped, to garnish

1 | Finely grate the cucumber and drain out any excess liquid. Set aside.

2 | Heat a small skillet on medium-high heat and add the mustard seeds and cumin seeds. Dry-roast the spices until they become slightly golden brown and fragrant.

3 | Remove the seeds from the heat. Once they cool, place them in a medium or large heavy mortar and pestle and grind into a fine powder. Alternatively, grind the spices in a clean coffee grinder on the finest setting.

4 | In a medium bowl, place the yogurt. Stir in the cucumber, mustard seeds, cumin seeds, and salt. Add the garlic paste and mix to combine the ingredients.

5 | Garnish with chili powder and cilantro. Chill in the refrigerator before serving. The raita will keep in the refrigerator for up to 2 days.

SWEET WHOLE SPICED PEAR, PLUM & CRANBERRY MURRABO

Sweet and laced with beautiful cardamom, cinnamon, and cloves, this Indian-spiced fruit jam known as murrabo single-handedly made me love Indian dals and beans for all their rustic flavor and heartiness. This modern recipe uses an uncommon combination of local late-summer and fall fruits and unquestionably makes its way onto my dining table and cheese boards during festive holidays. Choose fresh cranberries for their tartness and Bartlett pears for their buttery texture, refreshingly sweet quality, and firmness.

PREP TIME: 15 MINUTES

COOK TIME: 1 HOUR

YIELD: ABOUT 1 CUP

6 plums, peeled and finely cubed

2 ripe Bartlett pears, peeled and finely cubed

½ cup fresh cranberries

¼ cup raw cane sugar

1 tablespoon apple cider vinegar

½ teaspoon Indian chili powder

½ teaspoon cumin seeds

½ teaspoon sea salt

4 black peppercorns

4 green cardamom pods

3 cinnamon sticks

2 whole cloves

1 | In a small non-stick, heavy-bottomed pot on low heat, combine all the ingredients and cook, stirring occasionally, for up to 1 hour or until the mixture is soft, dry, and dark. All the moisture should be absorbed.

2 | Cool completely and transfer to a glass jar. This sweet chutney will keep in the refrigerator for up to 2 weeks. Serve with a complete Indian meal.

NOTE: Serve this beautiful and festive murrabo with a roast and all the trimmings during the holidays or anytime your savory main could use a sweet condiment on the side.

MANGO PEACH CHUTNEY

This chutney is traditionally made only with mangoes, but I add peaches to satisfy my late-summer peach obsession. A perfect balance of sweet, heat from chilies, and a touch of tang from chaat masala, this chutney is incredible with our Onion Kale Bhajias (page 99) served hot out of the fryer.

PREP TIME: 15 MINUTES

COOK TIME: 15 MINUTES

YIELD: 1½ CUPS

2 large peaches, peeled and finely cubed

1 large mango, peeled and finely chopped

¼ cup raw cane sugar

1 teaspoon coriander powder

½ teaspoon cumin seeds

½ teaspoon Indian chili powder

½ teaspoon sea salt

¼ teaspoon Tangy Chaat Masala (page 48)

1 tablespoon apple cider vinegar

1 teaspoon ginger paste

1 | In a small non-stick pot, combine the peaches, mangoes, sugar, coriander, cumin, chili powder, salt, and chaat masala and mix together. Stir in the apple cider vinegar and the ginger paste. Cook on medium-low heat, stirring occasionally, for 15 minutes or until the mixture softens and slightly caramelizes into a loose chutney.

2 | Remove from the heat to cool, then transfer to a glass jar. Keep in the refrigerator for up to 4 days. Serve with Onion Kale Bhajias (page 99).

NOTE: This chutney goes with any grilled specialties, such as Succulent Tandoori Chicken (page 180), Indian-Style Kebabs with Grilling Vegetables (page 187), or Tandoori-Spiced Paneer Kebabs with Grilling Vegetables (page 163), but is equally fantastic with a roast or grilled meats.

BASIC INDIAN SALAD & CONDIMENTS

Have you ever wondered why leafy green salads are rarely part of an Indian meal? The reason is because leafy greens such as collard greens, spinach, mustard greens, and others are usually cooked into a curry and served as part of the main meal. When it comes to Indian salads, known as kachumber, vegetables that lend cooling properties, such as cucumbers and tomatoes, are most often cut and simply served on a plate, ready to cool things off if (and when!) a tsunami of spice and flavor hits the palate. My memories of Indian dinners at friends' and relatives' homes are of spicy foods on the buffet table, but always coupled with fresh-cut tomatoes or a plate of refreshing cucumbers and radishes to help temper the spices. Here is a Basic Kachumber recipe, with some condiments that will round out any meal.

Basic Kachumber

PREP TIME: 25 MINUTES

YIELD: SERVES 4 TO 6

1 small red onion, to garnish

½ English cucumber, cut into ¼-inch cubes

12 cherry tomatoes, halved

6 radishes, sliced ⅛ inch thick

DRESSING

2 tablespoons apple cider vinegar

½ teaspoon Tangy Chaat Masala (page 48)

Pinch of Kashmiri chili powder (optional)

1 | Cut the onion in half lengthwise. Thinly slice the onion so the pieces are long and thin. Set aside as a garnish.

2 | In a large bowl, mix together the cucumbers, tomatoes, and radishes. Set aside.

3 | **FOR THE DRESSING:** In a small bowl, mix the dressing ingredients together. Add the dressing to the kachumber and toss well.

4 | Transfer the kachumber to a platter or serving plate and garnish with the red onions.

NOTE: This Basic Kachumber pairs with virtually any Indian meal, whether it's an elaborate feast or simple vegetarian dinner.

(continued)

Indian Salad Condiment Trifecta

PREP TIME: 15 MINUTES

YIELD: 2 CUPS

2 cups loosely packed fresh cilantro

1 medium tomato, finely cubed

1 medium red onion, finely chopped

1 | Rinse the cilantro in several changes of water to remove any grit or sand. Trim off the roots and discard; finely chop the cilantro.

2 | In a medium bowl, mix together the tomatoes, onions, and cilantro.

NOTE: This Indian-style salsa-like condiment is a classic combination of ingredients suited for Indian snacks or appetizers with its trifecta of cilantro, tomato and red onion. Use it as a topping on Savory Chaat Papri (page 91) or in an Indian-style omelet like Mom's Favorite Garam Masala Omelet (page 78). Always make this recipe fresh, right before use.

Pickled Red Onion & Green Chilies Condiment

PREP TIME: 10 MINUTES

YIELD: ¾ CUP

1 small red onion

3 small green chilies, finely chopped

½ cup apple cider vinegar

1 | Cut the onion in half lengthwise, then thinly slice the halves so the onion pieces are long and thin.

2 | In a small bowl or glass jar, place the onions and chilies. Pour the apple cider vinegar over top. This can be served immediately. It will keep in the refrigerator for 3 days and will turn a purply-pinkish hue as it marinates.

NOTE: This simple condiment adds a wow factor to non-vegetarian curries and dals—sprinkle a small spoonful of the vinegar with the red onions and green chilies on a curry just before eating and you'll experience sour, heat, and pungent tastes with every bite! Alternatively spoon on a small amount on the side of your plate or thali and periodically dip into it with your flatbread and curry when you want a soury-hot hit of flavor. Also try this condiment in an Indian-style burger—our Indian-Style Kebabs with Grilling Vegetables recipe (page 187) can be used to make burgers—or in a sandwich of your choice.

BEET, CARROT & CABBAGE KACHUMBER WITH GARAM MASALA VINAIGRETTE

In the 1990s, my mother and I would host an extravagant Valentine's Day Indian cooking class and dinner with a luxurious, romantic menu of Indian-inspired dishes laced with spices. Many spices are known to be natural aphrodisiacs that evoke the senses, with cardamom and saffron being the most alluring, so cooking an Indian dinner and weaving these sensual spices into the menu is a beautiful way to celebrate Valentine's Day. This gorgeous ruby-red beet kachumber was part of our Valentine's Indian-themed menu, and it presents beautifully over the holiday season too. The color is stunning and is a modern take on the traditional Indian kachumber.

PREP TIME: 30 MINUTES

YIELD: SERVES 4 TO 6

DRESSING

2 tablespoons apple cider vinegar

2 tablespoons freshly squeezed lemon juice

2 tablespoons olive oil

¾ teaspoon Warming Garam Masala (page 45)

½ teaspoon sea salt, or to taste

¼ teaspoon Indian chili powder

SALAD

2 cups finely shredded cabbage

2 Gala apples, peeled and finely grated

2 medium beets, peeled and finely grated

1 large carrot, peeled and finely grated

¼ cup finely chopped fresh mint

2 tablespoons finely chopped red onions (optional)

Fresh cilantro, finely chopped, to garnish

1 | **FOR THE DRESSING:** In a small bowl, combine all the dressing ingredients and whisk together. Set aside.

2 | **FOR THE SALAD:** In a large salad bowl, toss the cabbage, apples, beets, carrots, and mint together to mix well. Add the red onions and the dressing and toss well. Garnish with cilantro to taste and serve immediately.

TANDOORI-SPICED CHICKPEA SALAD WITH CILANTRO MINT YOGURT DRIZZLE

When soaking in the heat on the hottest summer days, I find myself, more often than not, craving cooling and lighter foods. For this reason, we created this recipe for our Indian Summer Entertaining cooking class to demonstrate a hearty salad option to pair with an Indian-style summer meal. For this salad, we season chickpeas with the Tandoori Marinade Spice Blend and sprinkle them on crispy kachumber, then generously layer with a cooling cilantro mint yogurt drizzle. I serve this salad chilled, though I like it served warm just as well. The contrast of warm chickpeas on a crispy cool salad somehow makes this feel more substantial as a whole meal in one.

PREP TIME: 20 MINUTES

COOK TIME: 10 MINUTES

YIELD: SERVES 4

CILANTRO MINT YOGURT DRIZZLE

½ cup finely chopped fresh cilantro

½ cup finely chopped fresh mint leaves

1 teaspoon garlic paste

1 green chili, finely chopped

¾ teaspoon raw cane sugar

½ teaspoon sea salt, or to taste

¾ cup dahi or Balkan-style yogurt

CHICKPEAS

1 tablespoon olive oil

2 teaspoons Tandoori Marinade Spice Blend (page 47)

2 cups channa (whole chickpeas), cooked, or one 19-ounce can, rinsed and drained

½ teaspoon garlic paste

¼ teaspoon sea salt, or to taste

SALAD

½ small head romaine hearts, finely chopped

1 medium tomato, finely cubed

¼ English cucumber, finely cubed

½ small red onion, finely chopped

Fresh cilantro, to garnish

1 | FOR THE CILANTRO MINT YOGURT DRIZZLE: Place all the ingredients except the yogurt in a blender and pulse until smooth. Transfer to a small bowl and stir in the yogurt.

2 | FOR THE CHICKPEAS: In a medium non-stick skillet on medium heat, gently heat the oil. Add the tandoori marinade spice blend and mix it with the oil. Add the chickpeas, garlic paste, and salt and mix well. Cook on medium heat for a couple of minutes or until the chickpeas are well coated with the spices and oil.

3 | FOR THE SALAD: On a large serving platter, arrange the romaine on the bottom layer. Layer the tandoori-spiced chickpeas on top, then sprinkle on the tomatoes, cucumbers, and onions. Drizzle with the cilantro mint yogurt drizzle. Garnish with cilantro to taste.

4 | INDIAN BRUNCH & EGGS

In India, breakfast can be as simple as a cup of tea with a savory biscuit, therefore much more emphasis is placed on brunch as a meal, with heartier and more satiating food items, sometimes including eggs. Always with a touch of masala, the recipes in this chapter show you how easy it is to create a showstopping Indian-style brunch perfect for a special weekend, to satisfy your morning spice craving, or when you feel like taking an easy morning to indulge over a steaming pot (or two!) of masala chai and the weekend newspaper.

INDIAN-SPICED DEVILED EGGS

Deviled eggs are so retro 1980s! *At the potlucks of my childhood, deviled eggs seemed to be a mainstay on picnic and dinner-party buffet tables, always front and center among a tuna bake, a pasta salad, and a plate of creamy mushroom vol-au-vents. And in typical Indian fashion, of course, we added spices to everything— including our deviled eggs! The first time I tasted my mother's Indian-style deviled eggs was when she hosted lunch for a large number of coworkers, who eagerly crammed into the house, hungry to taste Indian foods and flavors—most for the first time. To the deviled eggs, she added a dash of garam masala and a garnish of fresh cilantro, just perfect for those who weren't keen on too much spice. Now a family tradition, we make deviled eggs every springtime. This is a version of my mother's old '80s recipe, but I've added tandoori spices to change it up. The orange hue of the yolk, the white egg, and the fresh green garnishes uncannily match the colors of the Indian flag!*

PREP TIME: 40 MINUTES

YIELD: SERVES 4

6 hard-boiled eggs, shelled

¼ cup mayonnaise

1½ teaspoons Tandoori Marinade Spice Blend (page 47), or to taste

¼ teaspoon sea salt, or to taste

¼ cup finely chopped red onions

2 teaspoons Dijon mustard or yellow mustard

¼ red bell pepper, finely diced, to garnish

12 fresh cilantro leaves, to garnish

Kashmiri chili powder, to garnish

Green chilies, finely chopped, to garnish (optional)

1 | Halve the eggs lengthwise.

2 | In a medium bowl, scoop out the cooked egg yolks and mash with a fork.

3 | In a separate small bowl, add the mayonnaise and blend in the tandoori marinade spice blend and salt to taste. Mix in the onions and mustard. Add this mixture to the egg yolks and combine well. You can taste the filling at this point and adjust the seasoning if needed.

4 | Carefully and neatly spoon the mixture into each hard-boiled egg white and arrange the deviled eggs on a serving plate. Garnish with red peppers, cilantro, chili powder, and green chilies.

NOTE: To hard boil eggs, place eggs in a pot in a single layer and cover with cold water. Bring the water to a boil. Once the water is at a rolling boil, remove the pot from the stove, cover with a lid, and let stand for 12 minutes. Rinse with cool water to prevent a green or gray ring forming around the yolk. On a cutting board, crack the egg shell on all sides. Starting from the bottom of the egg, gently remove the shell; the rest should then peel off easily.

ANDA BHURJI

Scrambled eggs for breakfast are enjoyed around the world, with the Indian version being anda bhurji (anda is "eggs" and bhurji means "scrambled" in Hindi), and it's the way we enjoy scrambled eggs at home. With green chilies, fresh fenugreek, cumin, turmeric, and garam masala, anda bhurji has the right combination of ingredients that make it distinctly Indian. Instead of toast, serve anda bhurji with fresh hot chapatis or paranthas, with pickles on the side and a fresh chutney, such as Hot Chili Tomato Chutney (page 55). Although I normally eat these scrambled eggs hot out of the skillet, leftovers can keep in the refrigerator for up to 1 day. They're delicious when eaten cold too, with chapatis hot off the grill.

PREP TIME: 25 MINUTES

COOK TIME: 15 MINUTES

YIELD: SERVES 4

1 tablespoon ghee

¼ teaspoon cumin seeds

½ cup finely chopped onions

1 cup finely chopped cremini mushrooms

½ teaspoon garlic paste

½ teaspoon ginger paste

1 cup finely chopped fresh fenugreek leaves

½ cup finely chopped tomatoes

1 to 2 small green chilies, finely chopped, to taste

1 teaspoon coriander powder

½ teaspoon sweet paprika

¼ teaspoon cumin powder

¼ teaspoon turmeric powder

Pinch of Indian chili powder

4 large eggs

½ teaspoon sea salt

½ teaspoon Warming Garam Masala (page 45)

Fresh cilantro, finely chopped, to garnish

1 | In a medium or large non-stick skillet on medium-high heat, melt the ghee. Add the cumin seeds and fry for 15 to 30 seconds, until light golden brown and fragrant. Add the onions and cook for 3 to 4 minutes, until softened and translucent.

2 | Reduce the heat to medium. Add the mushrooms, garlic paste, and ginger paste and cook for a couple of minutes. Add the fenugreek and cook for a couple of minutes, until wilted. Add the tomatoes and green chilies to taste, and mix together. Sprinkle in the coriander, paprika, cumin powder, turmeric, and chili powder. Stir to combine and cook for a minute.

3 | In a medium bowl, crack in the eggs and whisk until combined. Mix in the salt and the garam masala.

4 | Adjust the heat to medium-high. Pour the eggs into the skillet and, using a flat utensil, move the eggs across the bottom of the pan, combining with the fenugreek mixture and to form soft "clouds." Cook for a few minutes or until eggs are cooked to the desired consistency. Transfer to a serving dish and garnish with cilantro to taste.

MOM'S FAVORITE GARAM MASALA OMELET WITH GHEE-FRIED TOAST

When we were kids, *my favorite memory of camping was waking up to the campsite breakfast. As I peeked out of the tent, the smell of breakfast encircled the campsite and filled the cool morning air with the gentle aroma of the garam masala used to season our morning eggs. My father's camping breakfast specialty was ghee-fried toast, where toast was drizzled with ghee and pressed in a frying pan over the gas camp stove. What started out as a camping treat became the perfect accompaniment to my mother's favorite omelet, which is simple and tasty with just the basics—onion, cilantro, tomato, green chilies, and garam masala—and can be enjoyed anytime, any day.*

PREP TIME: 15 MINUTES

COOK TIME: 15 MINUTES

YIELD: SERVES 1

TOPPING

1 teaspoon ghee

¼ cup finely chopped onions

¼ cup finely chopped tomatoes

¼ teaspoon Kashmiri chili powder

Pinch of sea salt

GHEE-FRIED TOAST

1 to 2 teaspoons ghee, for frying

2 slices bread

OMELET

2 eggs

1 small green chili, finely chopped

12 fresh cilantro leaves, plus extra to garnish

Pinch of Indian chili powder

Salt and freshly ground black pepper, to taste

1 teaspoon ghee

Warming Garam Masala (page 45), to garnish

1 | FOR THE TOPPING: In a medium non-stick skillet on medium heat, melt the ghee. Add the onions and fry for a couple of minutes, until they are translucent. Add the tomatoes and cook for another couple of minutes. Sprinkle in the chili powder and a pinch of salt. Mix until combined, then transfer the topping mixture to a bowl or plate and set aside.

2 | FOR THE GHEE-FRIED TOAST: Heat a medium non-stick skillet on medium-high heat and add 1 to 2 teaspoons ghee. Once the ghee is melted, add the bread and gently fry it in the skillet. Using a flat spatula, apply pressure to toast the bread and continue to fry, flipping, until the bread is golden brown on all sides. Transfer the toast to a plate.

3 | FOR THE OMELET: In a medium bowl, whisk together the eggs, green chilies, cilantro, and chili powder. Add salt and pepper to taste. Set aside.

4 | To the skillet, add 1 teaspoon of ghee and let melt. Add the egg mixture and spread evenly to make a thin crepe. Cook for 1 minute, until light golden brown, then flip over and cook for a few seconds until the omelet is cooked.

5 | Transfer the omelet to a plate and sprinkle the topping evenly on top. Garnish with a sprinkle of garam masala and cilantro as desired and serve with ghee-fried toast.

NOTE: This recipe easily batches, so scale the topping according to how many people you are serving. Make the omelets per person as required. Serve with Hot Chili Tomato Chutney (page 55).

BESAN PUDLA

For my weekend brunch table, *I often find myself making these Indian-style savory vegetable pancakes. They are hearty, protein-packed with chickpea flour, loaded with vegetables, and full of flavor, especially when topped with a fresh chutney. But it's the frilly, crispy little edges that keep me coming back for more! A few years ago, we were invited to collaborate with the chefs at the Art Gallery of Ontario for a presentation on Indian cooking when the exhibit* Maharaja: The Splendour of India's Royal Courts, *came to Canada. We made these simple chickpea-based pancakes, which were dressed up for the occasion into blinis topped with cilantro and chutney garnishes. Either served as a savory appetizer or for a hearty brunch, these pancakes are easy and delicious and can be enjoyed any time of day.*

PREP TIME: 25 MINUTES

COOK TIME: 45 MINUTES

YIELD: 12 PANCAKES

1 cup chickpea flour (gram flour or besan), sifted

½ cup rice flour, sifted

½ cup fine semolina (suji)

3 eggs

1⅔ cups water

2 teaspoons coriander powder

1¾ teaspoons sea salt, or to taste

1 teaspoon cumin powder

1 teaspoon turmeric powder

½ teaspoon Indian chili powder

2 cups finely chopped kale

1 cup finely chopped onions

¼ cup finely chopped fresh cilantro

1 to 2 small green chilies, finely chopped, to taste

Sunflower oil, for shallow frying

1 | In a large bowl, combine the flours and semolina. In a separate medium bowl, whisk the eggs, then add the water and stir in the coriander, salt, cumin, turmeric, and chili powder. Add the egg mixture to the flour mixture and whisk together to make a smooth batter.

2 | Add the kale, onions, cilantro, and green chilies. Mix to combine.

3 | In a large non-stick skillet on medium-high heat, heat 1 to 2 teaspoons oil and coat the pan evenly. Ensure the skillet is hot, then add ⅓ cup of pancake batter to the hot skillet and spread out thinly and evenly using the back of a spoon. Cook for a couple of minutes, until the edges of the pancake become frilly and crispy. Flip and cook on the other side until golden brown, then transfer the pancake to a plate.

4 | Continue with the remaining batter until all the pancakes are cooked.

NOTE: A host of different chutneys serve well with these pancakes, with the most popular being Hot Chili Tomato Chutney (page 55), Minty Green Cilantro Chutney (page 53), and Mango Peach Chutney (page 62). If you wish to make this recipe vegan, omit the eggs and add a little extra water (about ¼ cup) to thin out the batter. For a variation, use fresh fenugreek leaves or spinach in lieu of kale.

INDIAN-STYLE BAKED EGGS

When I was young, *brunch was nothing like the haute brunch options available*
today. There were pancakes and French toast, but never did I have baked eggs
for brunch. Several years ago, I tasted baked eggs on a trip to New York City and
became inspired to create this brunch recipe—I've been making it ever since. This is
an Indian-inspired recipe with leeks and cherry tomatoes and the option to use paneer
or goat cheese. Choose a premium-quality goat cheese for best results. And while
I mostly make this dish for brunch, it's a great gourmet lunch option when baked
in individual ramekins, or an easy dinner.

PREP TIME: 20 MINUTES

COOK TIME: 25 MINUTES

YIELD: SERVES 4

2 tablespoons olive oil, divided

¼ teaspoon cumin seeds

2 cups finely chopped leeks

⅓ cup finely chopped red onions

½ teaspoon coriander powder

¼ teaspoon Indian chili powder

¼ teaspoon turmeric powder

¼ teaspoon cumin powder

¼ teaspoon sea salt, or to taste

12 cherry tomatoes, halved

⅓ cup crumbled paneer or goat
cheese

6 eggs

Sea salt and freshly ground black
pepper, to taste

Warming Garam Masala (page 45),
to garnish

Fresh cilantro, finely chopped,
to garnish

Green chilies, finely chopped,
to garnish (optional)

1 | Preheat the oven to 425°F.

2 | In a medium non-stick skillet on medium heat, heat 1 tablespoon oil. Add
the cumin seeds and fry for a minute, until the seeds are lightly golden brown.
Add the leeks and onions and cook for a couple of minutes, until they become
fragrant and the onions glisten. Sprinkle in the coriander, chili powder,
turmeric, cumin, and salt. Cook for a minute, until the spices become fragrant.
Add the cherry tomatoes and continue to cook for a minute.

3 | In a medium casserole or baking dish or a small Dutch oven, add the
remaining 1 tablespoon oil and spread evenly to coat the bottom of the dish.
Transfer the leek, onion, and tomato mixture to the baking dish and spread
out evenly. Sprinkle on the paneer. Using the back of a wooden spoon, create
six indentations or a small well for each egg to sit in. Crack the eggs and place
one in each indentation.

4 | Place the baking dish on a larger rimmed baking sheet. Pour hot water
onto the baking sheet until it is about ½ inch up the side of the baking dish,
to create a bain marie. Carefully place in the center of the oven and bake for
15 minutes or until the egg yolks set.

5 | Season with salt and pepper to taste. Garnish with a sprinkle of garam
masala, cilantro, and green chilies to taste.

NOTE: For a delicious and heartier variation, substitute the
leeks with 2 cups finely chopped broccoli florets.

CHAI-SPICED APPLE BUCKWHEAT PANCAKES WITH MAPLE CREAM

The inspiration for this recipe comes from the ginger chai apple crepes that we often serve for dessert in our cooking classes. My mother stews the apples with shreds of ginger and a sprinkle of chai masala and cooks the apples until caramelized. For this recipe I adopted my mother's chai-spiced stewed apples as the pancake topping with clouds of whipped cream and pure maple syrup to serve as a brunch item that has a sweet, perfumy Indian touch!

PREP TIME: 30 MINUTES

COOK TIME: 30 MINUTES

YIELD: 10 TO 12 PANCAKES

PANCAKE BATTER

2 eggs

1 cup 2% or whole milk

2 tablespoons sunflower oil, plus extra for frying

1 cup buckwheat flour

½ cup all-purpose flour

2 teaspoons raw cane sugar

2 teaspoons Perfumy Chai Masala (page 46)

1 teaspoon baking powder

1 teaspoon baking soda

½ teaspoon sea salt

CHAI-SPICED APPLES

1 tablespoon ghee or unsalted butter

1 teaspoon pure maple syrup, plus extra to serve

3 Gala apples, peeled and thinly sliced

1 teaspoon Perfumy Chai Masala (page 46)

1 tablespoon water

2 teaspoons finely shredded gingerroot, plus extra to garnish

MAPLE CREAM

1 cup whipping cream

2 tablespoons pure maple syrup, plus extra for serving

1 | FOR THE PANCAKE BATTER: In a large bowl, whisk together the eggs, milk, and oil. Stir in the flours, sugar, chai masala, baking powder, baking soda, and salt. Set the mixture aside for 10 minutes to rest.

2 | FOR THE CHAI-SPICED APPLES: In a medium non-stick skillet on medium heat, melt the ghee. Add the maple syrup and stir to combine. Add the apples and sprinkle in the chai masala. Add the water and ginger. Stir and cook for 5 to 8 minutes, until the apples are caramelized and soft.

3 | FOR THE MAPLE CREAM: In a medium or large bowl, place the whipping cream. Using an electric hand blender or immersion blender, whip into soft peaks. Gently fold in the maple syrup and set aside in the refrigerator.

4 | Heat a large non-stick skillet on medium-high. Add 1 teaspoon oil or as much as necessary to coat the bottom of the skillet. Add ¼ cup of the pancake batter and spread out evenly on the surface of the pan. Cook for a couple of minutes, until bubbles start to appear on the surface. Flip over and cook on the other side until golden. Transfer to a plate and continue to cook the remaining batter.

5 | Place pancakes on individual plates to serve, topped with chai-spiced apples, a dollop of maple cream, and a drizzle of maple syrup. Garnish with extra ginger to taste.

5

INDIAN STREET FOODS & SAVORY APPETIZERS

In Indian cities and towns, street food is everywhere, as mass numbers of people are always on the move, needing quick pick-up foods while in transit to their next destination. (You'll notice I don't say "takeout" here, as the foods are eaten on the spot, not brought home.) Street food is often like a mini meal, loaded with multiple layers of bold flavors. Freshness comes by way of onions and chutneys, and savory texture comes from something crispy, deep-fried, or crunchy. The street-food recipes in this chapter can be served family-style or as upscale plated appetizers; some are Indian-inspired, offering new takes on the classics, while others are very traditional. Satiating, textured, and full-flavored, these recipes have two more things in common—they're mouthwatering and delicious!

HOMEMADE BESAN SEV

Midafternoon is the call for Indian teatime, when it's customary to have a steamy, soothing cup of masala chai to take a pause in the day and to socialize or connect with a relative, friend, or colleague. Often teatime comes with a savory snack such as sev, this deep-fried spicy noodle snack. Street-food vendors serve it in a paper cone, which is how I remember it from my visit to Mount Abu and to Juhu Beach in Mumbai.

PREP TIME: 10 MINUTES

COOK TIME: 15 MINUTES

YIELD: 2 CUPS

1 cup chickpea flour (gram flour or besan)

1 teaspoon sea salt

¼ teaspoon black pepper powder

¼ teaspoon turmeric powder

Pinch of Indian chili powder

Pinch of asafoetida

2 tablespoons water

2 tablespoons sunflower oil, plus extra for deep-frying

1 | In a medium bowl, sift in the chickpea flour and sprinkle in the salt, black pepper, turmeric, chili powder, and asafoetida. Mix to combine. Add the water, first stirring the dough together and then kneading it, then add the 2 tablespoons of oil and continue kneading so the result is a firm dough.

2 | Using a sev maker, select a disk template with small holes to make the crispy sev (noodles). Place the sev dough in the sev maker and secure the lid tightly. (If a sev maker is not available, a useful and quick hack is to use a pizza cutter to create sev noodles. Divide the sev dough into eight even-sized balls. Then roll out each ball on a pastry board—this may require a bit of oil to prevent sticking to the rolling pin—as thinly as possible. Using a pizza cutter, cut the dough into very thin strips.)

3 | Line a large plate or tray with paper towel.

4 | Fill a small kadhai or wok with oil 2 inches deep. Heat the oil on medium-high. Using the hand crank of the sev machine, slowly release a few noodles to test if the oil is hot enough for frying. If it is, the sev should quickly rise to the surface. Lower the heat to medium, as the thin sev will cook quickly (and can burn). Proceed to crank out more noodles, filling up the kadhai. (If you used a pizza cutter to cut the dough into thin strips, use a fork to gently lift the strips and fry them in the hot oil.)

5 | Fry until the noodles are golden brown, flipping them with a fork or a stainless-steel slotted spoon or frying strainer. Remove and drain on the paper-towel-lined plate or tray. Continue with the remaining sev dough, frying a small amount at a time. You may need to turn the heat back to medium-high. If it gets too hot, lower the heat back down to medium.

6 | Cool the sev completely before breaking into smaller pieces. Sev will keep in an airtight container for a couple of days, or serve immediately on top of Indian snacks and appetizers such as Savory Chaat Papri (page 91).

MASALA MAKAI

Corn is ubiquitous in India, *turning up in so many recipes because maize is India's third-most grown grain after rice and wheat. Corn is much loved all over the subcontinent, where chilies, chaat masala, lime, and salt are liberally sprinkled on top of freshly roasted corn by roadside vendors. This corn recipe, a favorite of my maternal grandfather, calls for sweet corn off the cob, where the kernels are sautéed with masala and generously topped with garnishes such as coconut, cilantro, and sev and drizzled with both Minty Green Cilantro Chutney (page 53) and Sweet & Tangy Tamarind Date Chutney (page 54). We hope that as soon as the newest local corn crop comes into season, this is the recipe you will turn to first. Undoubtedly, it's the one we'll be swooning over too!*

PREP TIME: 20 MINUTES

COOK TIME: 10 MINUTES

YIELD: SERVES 2 TO 4

3 ears fresh sweet corn, husks removed, or 2 cups frozen sweet corn niblets, thawed

1 tablespoon coconut oil

1 teaspoon brown mustard seeds

10 fresh curry leaves

1 teaspoon coriander powder

1 teaspoon sea salt, or to taste

½ teaspoon cumin powder

¼ teaspoon Indian chili powder

¼ teaspoon turmeric powder

¼ cup dried desiccated coconut, unsweetened

2 tablespoons peanuts, coarsely ground

GARNISHES

1 small red onion, finely chopped

Fresh cilantro, finely chopped

Minty Green Cilantro Chutney (page 53)

Sweet & Tangy Tamarind Date Chutney (page 54)

Homemade Besan Sev (page 88)

4 lime wedges (optional)

1 | On a cutting board, cut the corn along its core to remove the kernels. Set aside.

2 | In a medium non-stick pot on medium-high heat, heat the oil. Add the mustard seeds and fry for 15 to 30 seconds or until they begin to pop. Add the curry leaves and fry until they curl and glisten in the oil.

3 | Reduce the heat to medium and add the corn kernels. Sprinkle in the coriander, salt, cumin, chili powder, and turmeric and mix. Cook on medium heat until the corn is tender, about 10 minutes. Fold in the coconut and peanuts.

4 | Transfer to individual bowls and garnish with red onions and cilantro to taste. Top with the chutneys, and the sev for a crunchy garnish. Serve with a lime wedge on the side.

ONION KALE BHAJIAS

I first ate these deep-fried onion fritters during one of my many trips to England to visit my extended family. Every time we went for a visit, my grandparents, uncles, and aunts would take us to the same famous Indian vegetarian restaurant in Wembley after shopping. The place was a bustling snacks and drinks café where you took a ticket and excitedly waited for your number to be called out to get served. Soon thereafter, the hot snacks—including these savory fritters—were delivered to the table with lassi and an array of fresh chutneys.

In the U.K., most of the restaurant or pub versions of these fritters are made with long slices of onion, creating lacey, abstract, and irregular bhajias (often called bhajis in England) when dipped into the chickpea-based batter and then fried. They are most often served with a sweet mango chutney, which complements the spiciness. This recipe is based on my mother's bhajia recipe but is reminiscent of those fritters I remember from my childhood, so I've left the onions long and thinly sliced. I've added green kale, as I love to squeeze in leafy greens wherever I can, and in this case it's a welcome addition, adding more body to the bhajias.

Gluten-free and vegan, these bhajias should be served hot out of the fryer for maximum flavor, so be sure to prepare the mango chutney in advance.

PREP TIME: 25 MINUTES

COOK TIME: 25 MINUTES

YIELD: 14 TO 18 BHAJIAS

2 medium onions

1 cup finely chopped green kale

2 tablespoons finely chopped fresh cilantro

¾ cup chickpea flour (gram flour or besan), sifted

¼ cup rice flour

1 teaspoon kasoori methi (dried fenugreek leaves)

¾ teaspoon sea salt

½ teaspoon coriander powder

½ teaspoon cumin powder

¼ teaspoon Indian chili powder

1 | Slice the onions in half lengthwise. Thinly slice each half so the onion pieces are long and thin. With a clean tea towel or paper towel, pat the kale and cilantro to remove any excess moisture.

2 | In a medium mixing bowl, mix together the flours, kasoori methi, salt, coriander, cumin, chili powder, turmeric, and baking soda. Add the water and whisk to remove any lumps from the batter.

3 | Add the onions, kale, cilantro, and green chilies. Mix to combine.

4 | Line a dish or plate with a few sheets of paper towel to drain the oil from the bhajias.

(continued)

6 | For each samosa, use two strips of phyllo pastry. Place one strip of the pastry on the board and, using a pastry brush, spread some oil on this first layer. Then lay a second strip of phyllo on top. Take a couple of tablespoons of cooled samosa filling and place it at the top of the layered phyllo strip. Taking the top left corner, "swing" it across so it falls on the right side of the strip. Now pull the top right corner down and across to meet the left side of the strip. From here, you can start to form the equilateral triangle by continuing to fold it down, tucking in any loose ends until you reach the bottom of the pastry.

7 | Place the samosa on a baking sheet and continue with the rest of the phyllo pastry and filling (if you have any phyllo pastry left over, store it in the refrigerator and use it for an appetizer).

8 | Brush the tops of the samosas with oil, then bake for about 15 minutes or until flaky and golden brown. Serve with the chutney.

TANDOORI-SPICED FISH PAKORAS

My family is blessed to have the influence of so many talented women who are exceptional cooks and inspirational mentors. When visiting our aunt Urmila in England years ago, we were welcomed into her home in a gesture of true Indian hospitality: a full-service meal with appetizers, chutneys, biryanis, curries, and flatbreads. Everything was served at once to be eaten and enjoyed together. On this particular visit, in true British fashion, it was the aroma of fried fish that filled the air. For an appetizer, she made a delicious tempura fish paired with a tomato-based condiment. Some food memories are unforgettable, and this was certainly one of them. For so many years, that combination of fried fish and a tomatoey dipping sauce never left my mind. This tandoori-spiced fish pakora recipe is inspired by this food memory, and for this reason, it is compulsory to serve these with our Hot Chili Tomato Chutney (page 55)—and none other!

PREP TIME: 20 MINUTES, PLUS 5 MINUTES RESTING

COOK TIME: 20 MINUTES

YIELD: 16 TO 20 PAKORAS

½ pound filet wild-caught haddock

2 teaspoons Tandoori Marinade Spice Blend (page 47)

¼ teaspoon sea salt

PAKORA BATTER

⅔ cup chickpea flour (gram flour or besan), sifted

3 tablespoons cornstarch

½ teaspoon Tandoori Marinade Spice Blend (page 47)

¼ teaspoon sea salt

¼ teaspoon baking powder

¼ teaspoon baking soda

½ cup cold water

Sunflower oil, for deep-frying

Pinch of sea salt (optional)

Hot Chili Tomato Chutney (page 55), for serving

Lemon wedges, to garnish

1 | Cut the fish into 1 × 1½-inch bite-sized pieces and place in a medium bowl. Sprinkle in the tandoori marinade spice blend and salt. Mix well and refrigerate.

2 | **FOR THE PAKORA BATTER:** In a medium bowl, mix together all the ingredients to make a medium-thick batter—it should stick to the fish pieces and coat them well. Allow the batter to rest for 5 minutes. Add the marinated fish pieces to the batter and coat well.

3 | Fill a kadhai, wok, or deep-fryer with oil 2 inches deep, and heat the oil on medium-high. Test the oil temperature by dropping a little batter into the oil; when the batter floats immediately to the top, the oil is ready. Fry a few pakoras at a time, cooking for 4 to 5 minutes, until golden brown on all sides. Drain on paper towel. If you like, sprinkle the pakoras with a pinch of sea salt.

4 | Serve hot with hot chili tomato chutney and lemon wedges on the side.

6 | LENTILS & BEANS

The top lentil producers in the world are Canada and India, in that order. Indians make up about 70% of the world's vegetarian population, so Indian cuisine is well versed in cooking with pulses, as this is the main source of protein for vegetarians in India. Subsequently, almost every Indian meal, even non-vegetarian ones, are served with some form of lentils or beans. The recipes in this chapter visit different regions of India, inviting you to experience cooking with pulses in deliciously different ways.

KALE & BLACK-EYED PEAS

In 1993, when my mother started teaching her cooking classes, she called her venture Healthy Gourmet Indian Cooking, known to us by the abbreviation HGIC. This recipe is an HGIC original featured in the lentils and beans session, and we've been cooking it ever since. As our cooking classes evolved, we taught more intensive lentil and bean curry workshops as a way to boost interest in plant-based proteins and demonstrate how to cook them in an Indian way. This dish is traditionally made with just black-eyed peas all on their own, but my mother's rendition includes greens, making it a great meal in one.

PREP TIME: 15 MINUTES,
PLUS OVERNIGHT SOAKING

COOK TIME: 1 HOUR
15 MINUTES

YIELD: SERVES 4

1 cup black-eyed peas (whole), dried

4 cups water, plus extra if necessary

1½ teaspoons sea salt, divided

1 tablespoon sunflower oil

½ cup finely chopped onions

1 medium fresh tomato, chopped, or 1 tablespoon crushed tomatoes

1½ teaspoons coriander powder

½ teaspoon cumin powder

½ teaspoon turmeric powder

¼ teaspoon Indian chili powder

1 teaspoon garlic paste

2 cups finely chopped green kale

1 teaspoon kasoori methi (dried fenugreek leaves)

Fresh cilantro, finely chopped, to garnish

1 | In a medium bowl, rinse the black-eyed peas in two to three changes of warm water. Cover with fresh warm water and soak overnight.

2 | Rinse and drain the peas in another couple of changes of warm water, then place in a medium pot along with 4 cups water and 1 teaspoon salt. Cook on medium-high for 10 minutes, then reduce the heat to medium and simmer, partially covering with a lid. Cook for 40 minutes or until tender.

3 | In a separate medium non-stick pot on medium-high heat, heat the oil. Add the onions and cook until soft and golden brown, 5 to 10 minutes. Lower the heat to medium-low, then add the tomatoes and sprinkle in the coriander, cumin, turmeric, chili powder, and remaining ½ teaspoon salt. Add the garlic paste and stir to combine. Add the kale and cook for 5 to 7 minutes or until slightly wilted.

4 | Stir in the cooked black-eyed peas along with their cooking liquid. Add ½ cup water if they start to dry out. Sprinkle in the kasoori methi. Cover and simmer for 10 to 15 minutes or until the black-eyed peas are very tender and the spices have mixed in thoroughly. It should have a soupy consistency.

5 | Transfer to a serving dish and garnish with cilantro to taste.

NOTE: Feel free to use spinach, rapini, or fresh fenugreek leaves as a substitute for kale. Black-eyed peas can also be cooked in a pressure cooker in 10 minutes.

INSTANT POT MASOOR DAL SOUP WITH BROCCOLI

I've had a few interesting conversations with my mother about the use of broccoli in Indian cuisine. I've always insisted that you can add Indian spices to any vegetable and make a curry out of anything, but my mother tells me that using broccoli in Indian cooking is not typical, meaning it's not authentic!

To my understanding, broccoli is grown in India but is not ubiquitous like other cruciferous vegetables, such as cauliflower or mustard greens. Nonetheless, broccoli is still one of my favorite vegetables because of its texture, health benefits, and high protein content. For this reason, I've always been determined to use broccoli in my everyday Indian cooking. If you're like me and love broccoli too, then here is the perfect opportunity to cook broccoli in an Indian way.

One of our most beloved dal recipes is masoor dal (curried split red lentils), and many of the students in our cooking classes over the years will remember this dal either in the form of a soup or served thick with a sprinkle of garam masala on top of basmati rice. Easy to make and heavenly tasting with the nutty flavor from the ghee, this is my go-to comfort food with a hot chapati on the side.

PREP TIME: 10 MINUTES, PLUS 10 MINUTES INSTANT POT NATURAL PRESSURE RELEASE

COOK TIME: 25 MINUTES

YIELD: SERVES 4 TO 6

1 cup masoor dal (red lentils split and hulled), dried

1½ cups broccoli florets

6 cups water, divided, plus extra if necessary

1 teaspoon sea salt, plus extra to taste

1 tablespoon ghee

½ cup finely chopped onions

1 teaspoon coriander powder

1 teaspoon cumin powder

½ teaspoon turmeric powder

½ teaspoon Indian chili powder

Pinch of asafoetida

1 | In a medium bowl, rinse the lentils in four or five changes of water or until the water runs relatively clear. Drain.

2 | In an Instant Pot, combine the drained lentils, broccoli florets, and 3 cups water. Sprinkle in the salt. Take care to secure the lid correctly and be sure the pressure release valve is set to the sealing position. This is very important! The Instant Pot will register as "on." Adjust the setting to "pressure cook high" and set the time to 1 minute. It will take about 10 minutes for the Instant Pot to come to pressure.

3 | Once the pressure cooking is complete, the Instant Pot will begin the natural pressure release. Allow for 10 minutes of natural pressure release, then release the remaining pressure by carefully setting the pressure release valve to venting. Remember to wear an oven mitt or glove when venting and keep your hands and face away from the vent, as the steam is extremely hot and can burn! Handle the valve from the side, not from above or overhead. Open the lid only when it is safe to do so, checking that all the pressure has been released first.

4 | In a large non-stick pot on medium-high heat, melt the ghee. Add the onions and fry for a few minutes, until the onions are translucent and fragrant. Sprinkle in the coriander, cumin, turmeric, chili powder, and asafoetida. Stir in the garlic and ginger pastes and add salt to taste.

(continued)

1 teaspoon garlic paste

1 teaspoon ginger paste

Olive oil, to garnish

Warming Garam Masala (page 45), to garnish

Fresh cilantro, to garnish

5 | Add the cooked dal plus the remaining 3 cups water and simmer for 10 minutes. Adjust the seasoning according to your palate and add extra water if necessary to get the desired soup consistency.

6 | Ladle into soup bowls and garnish with a drizzle of oil, a sprinkle of garam masala, and some chopped cilantro to taste. Serve with Cumin-Scented Papads (page 211) on the side for dipping.

NOTE: An over-the-top garnish in lieu of olive oil is achar oil from the Matchstick Carrot & Green Chilies Achar (page 59), which adds a bold pop of flavor and pungency. Add a couple of drops or a generous drizzle, whichever you prefer.

SOUTH INDIAN SAMBAR

On our travels through Gujarat, we stayed in the village of Khergam, close to the bigger city of Surat. Life in Khergam is centered on food. In the early mornings, a farmer walks down the streets with a wagon full of freshly picked vegetables from the farm. In his loudest voice, he belts out, "Adu, lasan . . ." (meaning, "I have ginger, garlic . . ."), calling out all the vegetables and ingredients he has available to buy from his wagon. The ladies of the house where my brother and I were staying would congregate and scramble, checking what vegetable stocks they had on hand. On the spot, they reeled off recipe ideas and decided on the menu, running out to buy what they needed before the farmer headed off to the next street. One morning, they agreed the menu was going to be something special: South Indian sambar served with idli, which are pillowy rice cakes—an exotic dish to prepare in a Gujarati village! One taste of this sambar takes me back to my memorable travels to South India, where this is a daily staple.

For the vegetables, you can choose carrots, cauliflower, beans, or peas, but the signature ingredient for sambar is drumstick, a vegetable that hangs from the moringa tree. Drumsticks are typically available at South Asian grocery stores, but this recipe will still be tasty if you can't find them.

PREP TIME: 20 MINUTES, PLUS 2 HOURS SOAKING

COOK TIME: 55 MINUTES

YIELD: SERVES 4

1 cup toor dal (split and hulled pigeon peas), dried

4 cups water, plus extra if necessary

2 teaspoons sea salt, divided, plus extra to taste

2 tablespoons coconut oil

½ teaspoon brown mustard seeds

½ teaspoon cumin seeds

Pinch of asafoetida

8 to 10 fresh curry leaves

2 cups mixed vegetables (such as peeled carrots, cauliflower, green beans, peas, zucchini), cut into bite-sized pieces

1 drumstick, cut into 2-inch pieces (optional)

1 | In a medium bowl, rinse the dal in a few changes of water or until the water runs relatively clear. Cover with fresh warm water and soak for 2 hours. Drain.

2 | In a medium pot, combine the dal with 4 cups water and 1 teaspoon salt. Partially cover the pot and bring to a boil for 5 minutes, then reduce the heat to low and cook for 30 minutes or until the lentils are soft and cooked. Turn off the heat. Using a hand blender or immersion blender, puree until smooth.

3 | In a separate large heavy-bottomed pot on medium-high heat, heat the oil. Add the mustard seeds and cumin seeds and fry for a minute or until the mustard seeds begin to pop. Lower the heat to medium-low and add the asafoetida and curry leaves. Fry for a minute or until the curry leaves glisten.

4 | Add the mixed vegetables and drumstick. Sprinkle in the coriander, remaining 1 teaspoon salt, chili powder, cumin, and turmeric. Stir in the garlic and ginger pastes. Cover and cook until the vegetables are tender, 10 to 15 minutes, stirring occasionally.

(continued)

1½ teaspoons coriander powder

½ teaspoon Indian chili powder

½ teaspoon cumin powder

½ teaspoon turmeric powder

½ teaspoon garlic paste

½ teaspoon ginger paste

¼ cup unsalted crushed tomatoes

2 teaspoons jaggery or raw cane sugar, or to taste (optional)

¾ teaspoon concentrated tamarind paste

Fresh cilantro, to garnish

5 | Add the cooked dal, tomatoes, jaggery, and tamarind paste. Simmer for 10 minutes. Sambar should have a soupy consistency, so thin it out with a little extra water if necessary. Garnish with cilantro and adjust the salt to taste.

NOTE: How to eat the drumstick: If you're lucky enough to get a piece of drumstick in your bowl of sambar, pick it up with your hands and bite down on the exterior, scraping it along your teeth to remove the fleshy inner core. Once you've eaten all the core, discard the tough exterior for compost.

INSTANT POT WHOLE MASOOR DAL WITH FRESH TOMATOES

My first choice for a weeknight dal is masoor dal. It's a good source of protein, high in iron, and a fiber-rich food that's full of antioxidants, but I also enjoy its flavor and texture. This masoor dal is a little different and special with an added layer of freshness from the ripe tomato garnish. If it's fresh tomato season, this is definitely a recipe you should try! Serve hot with fresh chapatis and dahi on the side, with pickles and kachumber—a great-tasting, healthy lunch or dinner couldn't be simpler.

PREP TIME: 5 MINUTES, PLUS 5 MINUTES INSTANT POT NATURAL PRESSURE RELEASE

COOK TIME: 30 MINUTES

YIELD: SERVES 4

1 cup masoor (whole red lentils), dried

3 cups water, plus extra if necessary

1¼ teaspoons sea salt, divided, plus extra to taste

2 teaspoons ghee or sunflower oil

2 tablespoons unsalted crushed tomatoes

¾ teaspoon coriander powder

½ teaspoon cumin powder

½ teaspoon turmeric powder

¼ teaspoon Indian chili powder

½ teaspoon garlic paste

1 medium fresh tomato, finely chopped, to garnish

Fresh cilantro, finely chopped, to garnish

1 | In an Instant Pot, combine the masoor, 3 cups water, and 1 teaspoon salt. Take care to secure the lid correctly and be sure the pressure release valve is set to the sealing position. This is very important. The Instant Pot will register as "on." Adjust the setting to "pressure cook low" and set the timer for 9 minutes. Once the pressure cooking is complete, the Instant Pot will begin the natural pressure release. Allow for 5 minutes of natural pressure release, then release the remaining pressure manually by carefully setting the pressure release valve to venting. Always wear an oven mitt or glove when venting and keep your hands and face away from the vent, as the steam is extremely hot and can burn. Handle the valve from the side, not from above or overhead. Open the lid only when it is safe to do so, checking that all the pressure has been released first.

2 | In a separate medium non-stick pot on medium-high heat, heat the ghee. Add the crushed tomatoes and stir. Reduce the heat to medium-low and sprinkle in the coriander, cumin, turmeric, chili powder, and remaining ¼ teaspoon salt. Stir in the garlic paste and cook for a couple of minutes, until the spices become fragrant.

3 | Stir in the cooked masoor along with their cooking liquid and simmer on medium heat for 7 to 10 minutes or until the dal reduces. Add salt to taste and add extra water if necessary to get your desired consistency.

4 | Transfer to a serving dish and garnish with chopped tomatoes for freshness and cilantro to taste. Serve with a flatbread or plain boiled rice.

NOTE: To make this recipe without an Instant Pot, rinse the masoor in a few changes of warm water and soak the lentils for 3 hours. Rinse them again and drain. In a medium pot, combine the lentils with 3½ cups water and 1 teaspoon salt. Cook on medium-high for 10 minutes, then reduce the heat to medium and simmer for 30 minutes, partially covered. Continue with steps 2 to 4 to finish making the dal.

SPROUTED MOONG BEANS

Growing up, we had a tradition *affectionately known as Moong Mondays. Jokes aside, eating moong on Mondays has a true purpose. According to Ayurveda, moong beans are a powerful detoxifier, ridding the body's organs of the build-up of toxins, known as ama. Monday is a great day for detoxifying, as the weekends can be the time when we're more likely to indulge and let go of a healthy eating regimen. Sprouting moong beans is common in Indian cooking, offering more nutritional value to the already nutrient-dense moong bean. Time is the only factor to consider, as sprouting requires a minimum of 48 hours. If you're planning to serve sprouted moong beans on a Monday, start the sprouting process on the previous Friday, or Saturday at the latest.*

A couple of things to remember when sprouting: When rinsing the moong beans, it's important to drain the water and keep a moist paper towel or cheesecloth on top of the bowl and refresh it from time to time with a spritz of water if it dries out. Use a large bowl to allow for the moong beans to grow their sprouts, and place the bowl in a warm place in your kitchen—this is especially important in the cooler months.

PREP TIME: 10 MINUTES, PLUS OVERNIGHT SOAKING, PLUS 2 DAYS SPROUTING

COOK TIME: 25 MINUTES

YIELD: SERVES 4

1 cup moong beans (whole), dried

3 tablespoons sunflower oil

1 to 2 small green chilies, sliced lengthwise

2 teaspoons coriander powder

1 teaspoon sea salt, or to taste

1 teaspoon turmeric powder

½ teaspoon cumin powder

¼ teaspoon Indian chili powder

½ teaspoon garlic paste

¼ cup water

1 tablespoon finely shredded fresh gingerroot, to garnish

1 | In a large bowl, soak the whole moong beans in warm water overnight. Rinse them again in two to three changes of warm water, then completely drain the moong beans.

2 | Add the drained moong beans to a large bowl and cover the bowl with a moist paper towel or cheesecloth. Place the bowl in a warm place for 2 days, making sure the paper towel or cheesecloth is moist at all times. This will allow the moong beans to sprout.

3 | After 2 days, the moong beans should be sprouted! Once sprouted, the yield should be about 4 cups. Rinse and drain the sprouted moong beans to prepare them for cooking.

4 | In a large or medium non-stick pot or pan on medium heat, heat the oil. Add the green chilies and fry for 1 minute to release their flavor. Add the sprouted moong beans and sprinkle in the coriander, salt, turmeric, cumin, and chili powder. Add the garlic paste and mix well to combine.

5 | Add the water and cover with a lid. Cook on low heat for 15 minutes or until the beans are tender. Garnish with the ginger. Serve with Everyday Whole Wheat Chapatis (page 203), a vegetable curry of your choice, Basic Cooling Cucumber Raita (page 60), and Matchstick Carrot & Green Chilies Achar (page 59).

NOTE: These sprouted moong beans can also double up as a healthy lunch option! Serve them in a pita pocket with chopped tomatoes, lettuce, red onion rings, and a big dollop of raita.

PANTRY CHANNA MASALA

The back-to-school fall season *is always a busy time of year, when schedules become more rigid and life falls back to routine after a slower-paced summer. I created this easy version of a channa masala for nights when you're scratching your head figuring out the evening's dinner, or for when your refrigerator is only half full and you turn to your pantry for inspiration. I like to pair this channa with something that complements the tomato sauce well but is a low-carb, keto-friendly vegetable option. The spaghetti squash is a fantastic medium for a satiating and delicious Indian meal that's light and healthy.*

PREP TIME: 20 MINUTES

COOK TIME: 30 MINUTES

YIELD: SERVES 2 TO 4

SPAGHETTI SQUASH

2½ cups water

1 medium spaghetti squash, sliced in half lengthwise, seeded

2 tablespoons ghee or olive oil

¼ cup finely chopped fresh cilantro

½ teaspoon garlic paste

¼ teaspoon sea salt

1 | FOR THE SPAGHETTI SQUASH: In a medium pot, add the water and place the spaghetti squash skin side down in the pot. Leaving the lid ajar, cover and cook on medium-high heat for 30 minutes or until the squash is tender.

(continued)

4 | Reduce the heat to medium-low, stir in the tomatoes, and sprinkle in the cumin powder, remaining 1 teaspoon salt, turmeric, and chili powder. Add the garlic paste, stir to combine, and cook for a couple of minutes. Stir in the cooked beans, and add water if required to get the desired consistency. Simmer on low heat for a couple of minutes. Add the fresh tomatoes, green chilies, and salt to taste and gently simmer on medium heat for 10 to 15 minutes. Garnish with garam masala and cilantro to taste.

NOTE: You can reduce the cooking time for the beans by using a pressure cooker or Instant Pot. Soak the beans in warm water overnight, then cook the beans in a pressure cooker for 10 to 15 minutes. Always refer to the appliance user manual for correct cooking times, as they will vary.

Bottle gourd (lauki), zucchini, or butternut squash could be used as wonderful substitutions for the pumpkin in this recipe. Channa dal is commonly referred to as split Bengal gram.

INSTANT POT PANCH PHORAN CHANNA DAL WITH PUMPKIN

Panch phoran consists of five different spices *that deliver a distinctive punch of flavor—brown mustard seeds add a mild pungency; nigella seeds lend a delicious oniony flavor; fenugreek seeds give a touch of bitterness; cumin brings in warmth and earthiness; and fennel imparts a licorice-like sweetness. This Bengali Five Spice never fails to add excitement to a dish, and this channa dal preparation with pumpkin is no exception. Channa dal as a lentil has a wonderful hearty texture and can handle the bold flavors of panch phoran. When cooked in the Instant Pot, the panch phoran imparts its extraordinary flavor so impeccably well, I don't think I'll be eating channa dal any other way now!*

PREP TIME: 15 MINUTES, PLUS 10 MINUTES FOR INSTANT POT NATURAL PRESSURE RELEASE

COOK TIME: 20 MINUTES

YIELD: SERVES 4

1 cup channa dal (Indian chickpeas, split and hulled), dried

2 tablespoons sunflower oil

2 teaspoons Panch Phoran (page 49)

1 cup cubed peeled pumpkin

1 medium tomato, finely cubed

1¼ teaspoons sea salt, plus extra if necessary

½ teaspoon coriander powder

½ teaspoon cumin powder

½ teaspoon turmeric powder

¼ teaspoon Indian chili powder

½ teaspoon garlic paste

2 cups water, plus extra if necessary

Warming Garam Masala (page 45), to garnish

Fresh cilantro, to garnish

1 | In a medium bowl, rinse the channa dal in a few changes of warm water. Cover with fresh warm water and set aside to soak.

2 | Meanwhile, turn the setting of an Instant Pot to "sauté more." Heat the oil and sprinkle in the panch phoran. Fry the spices until the cumin seeds turn golden brown, the mustard seeds begin to pop, and the spices become fragrant.

3 | Lower the setting to "sauté less." Add the pumpkin and tomatoes and sprinkle in the salt, coriander, cumin, turmeric, and chili powder. Mix together, then stir in the garlic paste. Cook for a couple of minutes, until the spices become fragrant.

4 | Drain the dal and add it to the Instant Pot, gently folding to coat the dal with the spices. Add the 2 cups water.

5 | Take care to secure the lid correctly and be sure the pressure release valve is set to the sealing position. This is very important. The Instant Pot will register as "on." Adjust the setting to "pressure cook low" and set the timer for 3 minutes. Once the pressure cooking is complete, the Instant Pot will begin the natural pressure release. Allow for 10 minutes of natural pressure release, then release the remaining pressure manually by carefully setting the pressure release valve to venting. Always wear an oven mitt or glove when venting and keep your hands and face away from the vent, as the steam is extremely hot and can burn! Handle the valve from the side, not from above or overhead. Open the lid only when it is safe to do so, checking that all the pressure has been released first.

6 | Stir the dal, then thin out with extra water and adjust the salt if required.

7 | Transfer the dal to a serving dish and garnish with garam masala and cilantro to taste.

TARKA DAL MEDLEY

If you're like me and cook dal a few times a week, you can shake up your dal routine by mixing two or three dals together to create something new altogether. This is what my mother does to change things up, as a creative way to cook lentils. What's fun about cooking multiple dals together is that you can play with the textures of different varieties to create something new and exciting. In this recipe, we pair masoor dal (red split lentils) with split and hulled moong dal, which both impart a yellow color and melt together into a creamy texture. The addition of a third dal, channa dal, which retains its shape, gives you bites of full split lentils and balances the creaminess of the other two dals.

PREP TIME: 5 MINUTES,
PLUS 2 HOURS SOAKING

COOK TIME: 35 MINUTES

YIELD: SERVES 4

½ cup, masoor dal (red lentils split and hulled), dried

½ cup moong dal (split and hulled), dried

¼ cup channa dal (Indian chickpeas, split and hulled), dried

4 cups water, plus extra if necessary

1¾ teaspoons sea salt, divided, plus extra to taste

½ cup finely chopped onions

1½ teaspoons coriander powder

½ teaspoon cumin powder

½ teaspoon turmeric powder

¼ teaspoon Indian chili powder

½ teaspoon garlic paste

TARKA
2 tablespoons ghee

4 to 6 dried red chilies, or to taste

1 teaspoon cumin seeds

Pinch of asafoetida

Fresh cilantro, finely chopped, to garnish

1 | In a medium bowl, rinse all three types of dal together in a few changes of warm water or until the water runs relatively clear. Cover with fresh warm water and soak for 2 hours.

2 | Rinse and drain the soaked lentils and add them to a medium heavy-bottomed pot. Add 4 cups water, 1 teaspoon salt, and the onions. Partially cover and cook on medium-high for 10 minutes, then reduce the heat to medium and simmer for about 10 to 15 minutes or until the lentils are tender. Periodically check that there is enough water in the pot to fully cover the lentils when boiling, and add a little extra if necessary.

3 | Sprinkle in the coriander, remaining ¾ teaspoon salt, cumin, turmeric, and chili powder. Add the garlic paste and mix it into the dal. Simmer for 5 minutes.

4 | FOR THE TARKA: In a small skillet on medium-high heat, heat the ghee. Add the dried chilies to taste, cumin seeds, and asafoetida and fry until the chilies glisten and slightly expand and the cumin seeds become light golden brown and fragrant. Drizzle the tarka on top of the dal right before serving. Garnish with cilantro to taste.

NOTE: If you have fresh or dried curry leaves, you could also add 8 to 10 leaves to the tarka.

DAL MAKHANI

In 2017, I hosted an Indian cooking television series called Masala Magic Recipes. *In one episode, I demonstrated a special Punjabi menu in celebration of Vaisakhi (or Baisakhi), the annual Indian harvest festival that arrives in spring. I chose dal makhani as the main for this celebratory meal because it is the dal of dals! Simmered at length, naturally sweetened with caramelized onions, and lavishly rich with both ghee and cream, this dal has a full mouthfeel that's sure to please.* Makhani *is the Hindi word for a curry sauce cooked in rich butter or cream, so the name itself implies this dal's regal and indulgent nature. This dish is made using urad dal, also known as black gram dal or kaali dal. The dark dal color contrasted against the yogurt garnish and bright green cilantro leaves makes dal makhani one of the most attractive dals on a banquet table.*

PREP TIME: 5 MINUTES, PLUS OVERNIGHT SOAKING

COOK TIME: 1 HOUR 10 MINUTES

YIELD: SERVES 4

1 cup urad (whole), dried

3½ cups water, plus extra if necessary

1½ teaspoons sea salt, divided, plus extra to taste

3 tablespoons ghee

½ cup finely chopped onions

1 medium tomato, finely cubed, or 1 tablespoon unsalted crushed tomatoes

1 teaspoon coriander powder

¾ teaspoon cumin powder

½ teaspoon turmeric powder

¼ teaspoon Indian chili powder

1 teaspoon garlic paste

1 teaspoon ginger paste

½ cup half-and-half cream

¼ cup dahi or Balkan-style yogurt, room temperature, to garnish

Fresh cilantro, to garnish

1 | In a medium bowl, rinse the urad in a few changes of warm water. Cover with fresh warm water and soak them overnight.

2 | Rinse and drain the soaked urad and add them to a medium pot. Add 3½ cups water and 1 teaspoon salt and cook on medium-high for 10 minutes. Reduce the heat to medium and simmer, partially covered, for 25 to 30 minutes or until the urad are tender and cooked. Be sure there is enough water in the pot to fully cover the urad when cooking.

3 | In a separate medium non-stick pot on medium-high heat, heat the ghee. Add the onions and cook until softened and slightly golden brown, about 10 minutes. Reduce the heat to medium, add the tomatoes, and cook for 1 minute, stirring. Sprinkle in the coriander, cumin, turmeric, remaining ½ teaspoon salt, and chili powder and mix well to combine. Stir in the garlic and ginger pastes.

4 | Stir in the cooked urad along with their cooking liquid, cover, and simmer on medium heat for 10 minutes. Stir in the cream and cook for a couple of minutes, adding salt to taste and extra water if necessary to get the desired consistency. Continue to simmer for another 15 to 20 minutes or until the dal thickens up.

5 | In a small bowl, whisk the dahi until smooth, then drizzle as a garnish on top of the dal. Garnish with cilantro to taste.

NOTE: Cook the urad in a pressure cooker or Instant Pot to reduce the cooking time in this recipe. When using the pressure cooker, it is still mandatory to soak the urad, but the cook time will reduce to 10 to 15 minutes (depending on your pressure cooker). Always refer to the user manual to ensure you are using the pressure cooker correctly. Safety comes first!

7

| VEGETABLES

A visit to any outdoor market in India will show you vegetables bursting at the seams, creating a culinary kaleidoscope that makes these markets a vegetable lover's paradise. Adding to the excitement are all the vegetables that are grown on the subcontinent, such as snake gourd, bottle gourd (lauki or doodhi), red carrots, elephant foot yam, okra, Indian eggplants, fenugreek, and mustard greens—all just waiting to be cooked with spices. Vegetable curries are enjoyed in abundance and are served with every Indian meal. In this chapter, explore an array of our most loved Indian vegetable recipes using locally grown vegetables. Remember to eat in season for the ultimate taste and flavor.

ALOO METHI

My mother's go-to road-trip food is this savory potato recipe served with chapatis, homemade yogurt, and pickles. I remember stopping off, during road trips, in parks for lunch and having aloo methi alongside homemade sandwiches instead of rest-stop takeout. What makes aloo methi such a good road-trip food is that it packs well, does not require heating to taste great, and is absolutely delicious thanks to the bold fenugreek leaves. When eaten with chapatis and yogurt, the meal is satiating and definitely hits the spot. If no road trip is pending, not to worry, as this potato side dish will go with any dal or rustic Indian meal. I like to cook the potatoes a little longer on medium-high heat so they sear and turn golden brown, leaving crispy bits at the bottom of the pan. If you're anything like us, fighting over who gets the crispy potatoes always seems to be a thing!

PREP TIME: 15 MINUTES

COOK TIME: 20 MINUTES

YIELD: SERVES 4

2 large or 4 medium Russet potatoes, peeled

3 tablespoons sunflower oil

2 cups finely chopped fresh fenugreek leaves

1 teaspoon coriander powder

1 teaspoon cumin powder

½ teaspoon turmeric powder

¼ teaspoon Indian chili powder (add up to ½ teaspoon for more heat)

1¼ teaspoons sea salt, or to taste

1 | Slice the potatoes in half lengthwise, then continue to thinly slice in ⅛- to ¼-inch thick slices. Be sure that all the potatoes are of the same thickness so they cook at the same rate.

2 | In a large non-stick skillet on medium-high heat, heat the oil. Add the potatoes and fenugreek. Sprinkle in the coriander, cumin, turmeric, and chili powder, distributing the spices evenly over the potatoes. With a wide utensil or spatula, fold the potatoes so they are evenly coated with the spices and oil. Sprinkle in the salt and fold again.

3 | Cover with a lid and reduce the heat to medium-low. Cook the potatoes for 10 to 15 minutes or until they are softened, occasionally turning so they don't burn or stick to the bottom of the pan. If you want the potatoes to be slightly crispy, adjust the heat to medium-high toward the end of cooking and allow the potatoes to get golden brown. Serve with chapatis and dahi.

KASHMIRI DUM ALOO

For many years, my mother and I have been teaching private cooking classes with custom menus for our students who have special requests to learn very specific Indian dishes, whether it's to cater to a special diet or tailor a menu to someone's liking. One special inquiry I remember from many years ago was to teach a group of chefs in their commissary kitchen. Each chef submitted their requests for a custom menu, and one chef, Olivia, requested dum aloo, a Kashmiri preparation of boiled baby potatoes immersed in a delicious red tomato yogurt gravy. This potato curry is especially flavorful with a touch of tartness from the yogurt and a depth of spices that comes through the tomato curry. In this recipe, it's important to use Kashmiri chili powder, which will lend a beautiful red color to the curry sauce.

PREP TIME: 25 MINUTES

COOK TIME: 30 MINUTES

YIELD: SERVES 4

1½ pounds baby potatoes

3 tablespoons sunflower oil, divided

½ teaspoon brown mustard seeds

½ teaspoon cumin seeds

Pinch of asafoetida

¼ cup unsalted crushed tomatoes

1 teaspoon Kashmiri chili powder, or to taste

1 teaspoon sea salt, or to taste

1 teaspoon coriander powder

½ teaspoon cumin powder

¼ teaspoon turmeric powder

¾ cup warm water

¼ cup dahi or Balkan style yogurt, room temperature

Fresh cilantro, finely chopped, to garnish

1 | In a medium pot, add the potatoes and cover them with water. Partially cover the pot and cook the potatoes until they become tender. This usually takes about 15 minutes. Drain.

2 | Rinse the potatoes in cold water so they can be handled. Once the potatoes slightly cool in temperature, remove their skins. Using a fork, prick the potatoes to create small holes for the tomato gravy to seep in during the cooking process.

3 | In a medium non-stick skillet on medium-high heat, heat 2 tablespoons oil. Add the potatoes and gently fry them for a few minutes until they become golden. Set aside.

4 | In a medium non-stick pot on medium-high heat, heat the remaining 1 tablespoon oil. Add the mustard seeds and cumin seeds. Fry for 15 to 30 seconds or until the mustard seeds begin to pop. Add the asafoetida.

5 | Stir in the tomatoes and sprinkle in the chili powder, salt, coriander, cumin powder, and turmeric. Mix and cook for a couple of minutes. Reduce the heat to medium low.

6 | In a small bowl, whisk together the warm water and dahi and add it to the curry. Simmer for a couple of minutes, then add the baby potatoes. Stir to combine and adjust the salt, if necessary. Simmer for a few more minutes, until the result is a thick gravy. Garnish with cilantro to taste.

NOTE: To prevent the dahi or yogurt from curdling when adding it to this dish, first bring the dahi to room temperature, then whisk it in the warm water before adding it to the curry.

ALOO PANCH PHORAN

Roasted potatoes offer a comfort factor to any meal and never fail to please, especially when the potatoes are crispy with golden-brown edges, steaming hot, and fluffy in the middle. While this potato side dish will pair well with virtually any Indian meal, feel free to serve it whenever potatoes are needed for a side—it's delectably spiced so it easily gets along with foods from any cuisine. For this recipe, I suggest a slight modification to the panch phoran. I swap out the fenugreek seeds for kasoori methi (dried fenugreek leaves), as the fenugreek dried herb works far better in a dry dish than do the seeds, which are difficult to chew. If you haven't cooked with Bengali panch phoran yet, this recipe beckons you to give it a go—you'll be glad you did!

PREP TIME: 15 MINUTES

COOK TIME: 30 MINUTES

YIELD: SERVES 4

4 large Russet potatoes, peeled

1 teaspoon kasoori methi (dried fenugreek leaves)

½ teaspoon brown mustard seeds

½ teaspoon cumin seeds

½ teaspoon fennel seeds

½ teaspoon nigella seeds

2 tablespoons olive oil

½ teaspoon sea salt, or to taste

¼ teaspoon turmeric powder

Fresh cilantro, finely chopped, to garnish (optional)

1 | Preheat the oven to 425°F. Cut the potatoes into 1¼-inch cubes.

2 | In a small bowl, combine the kasoori methi, mustard seeds, cumin seeds, fennel seeds, and nigella seeds to make panch phoran for this dish.

3 | To a medium Dutch oven, baking dish, or sheet pan, add the potatoes, then drizzle with the olive oil and sprinkle with the panch phoran spices. Mix well, coating the potatoes with oil and spices evenly.

4 | Sprinkle the potatoes with the salt and turmeric. Toss again to coat well.

5 | Bake in the center of the oven for 25 minutes, occasionally flipping the potatoes so they get golden brown on all sides. If the potatoes are not cooked through, continue to bake for another 5 minutes. Garnish with a pinch of sea salt, if required, and with cilantro, if desired.

BAINGAN BHARTA

The use of eggplants in Indian cuisine is widespread. They are used in mixed vegetable curries, cooked with beans, steamed, and stuffed—such as in our Eggplant Ravaiya recipe (page 146). But perhaps the most famous and most loved way to prepare eggplant is in baingan bharta. Steamed or baked in the oven (or roasted over a flame to impart a smoky flavor), the eggplant is then mashed and cooked with cumin seeds and a dollop of ghee, simmered, and reduced. This, to me, is the most luxurious way to enjoy eggplants, especially when flaky paranthas are available on the side for dipping. For the bharta recipe, we favor Sicilian eggplant, known for its sweetness, mildness, and white flesh that can take up the Indian spices; otherwise, select the larger globe eggplant commonly found in the grocery store. Choose a fresh eggplant that's glossy, smooth, and free of wrinkles and indentations. A vibrant green stem is another indication of a fresh eggplant, which is extremely important for this recipe.

PREP TIME: 30 MINUTES

COOK TIME: 1 HOUR

YIELD: SERVES 4

2½ cups water

1 large Sicilian or globe eggplant

1 tablespoon ghee

1 teaspoon cumin seeds

½ cup finely chopped onions

1 tomato, finely chopped

1 small green chili, finely chopped

1 teaspoon coriander powder

¾ teaspoon sea salt, or to taste

½ teaspoon cumin powder

1 teaspoon garlic paste

Fresh cilantro, to garnish

1 | Pour the water into a medium pot. Place the eggplant in a steamer (or stainless-steel steaming basket) and set it in the pot. If you don't have a steamer, an alternative is to place a small inverted stainless-steel bowl on the bottom of the pot, fill the water around it, then place the eggplant on top. Partially cover, and cook on medium-high heat for 30 to 40 minutes or until the eggplant is soft enough to mash.

2 | Transfer the eggplant to a board and allow it to slightly cool so it can be handled. Then immediately peel off the skin and finely mash the eggplant.

3 | In a medium non-stick pot on medium-high heat, melt the ghee. Add the cumin seeds and fry for 15 to 30 seconds or until they become fragrant and light golden brown. Add the onions and fry for 7 to 10 minutes or until golden brown.

4 | Adjust the heat to medium and stir in the tomatoes and green chilies. Cook until the tomatoes are softened. Add the mashed eggplant and combine, then sprinkle in the coriander, salt, and cumin. Stir in the garlic paste and cook for 5 to 10 minutes, stirring. Adjust with extra salt, if required.

5 | Transfer to a serving dish and garnish with cilantro to taste. Serve as a vegetable side with another curry or dal.

NOTE: For an alternative cooking method, make slits in the flesh of the eggplant and roast on a baking sheet in a 400°F oven for 30 minutes. No salting or oil is required. Once the eggplant is roasted, peel the eggplant and mash it. Another option is to roast the eggplant over a low flame on the barbecue, which will lend a smoky flavor to this dish.

GUJARATI-STYLE SAMBHARO

A classic combination, shredded cabbage and carrots always make for a great vegetable side with any meal. You could call this an Indian version of coleslaw (without the creamy dressing!), but it's more like a warm Indian salad that's stir-fried with tempered mustard seeds. It's important not to overcook the cabbage and carrots to the point that they become wilted and reduced, which would cause the salad to lose its crunch and texture. For this recipe, I like green cabbage rather than purple, because the shreds become a beautiful golden hue from the turmeric. The result is a delicately spiced, gorgeous sunny salad that will brighten any plate.

PREP TIME: 20 MINUTES

COOK TIME: 10 MINUTES

YIELD: SERVES 4

1 tablespoon sunflower oil

1 teaspoon brown mustard seeds

2 medium carrots, peeled and grated

2 green chilies, sliced lengthwise (optional)

½ red bell pepper, sliced

¼ medium cabbage, finely shredded

1 teaspoon turmeric powder

1 teaspoon raw cane sugar

½ teaspoon sea salt

1 teaspoon freshly squeezed lemon juice

1 | In a large kadhai, wok, or non-stick pan on medium-high heat, heat the oil. Add the mustard seeds and fry for 15 to 30 seconds or until they begin to pop.

2 | Add the carrots, chilies, peppers, and cabbage and toss to mix together.

3 | Sprinkle in the turmeric, sugar, salt, and lemon juice.

4 | Mix well and stir-fry for a few minutes. Be sure not to overcook the vegetables. Serve as a delicious vegetable side for any meal.

NOTE: Although we suggest serving this warm, it can also be served cold with an Indian-style barbecue.

TRADITIONAL KERALAN AVIAL

Creamy with coconut, scented with curry leaves, and prepared with a variety of vegetables, this curry is one of the most loved South Indian vegetable specialties. We had the good fortune while traveling to learn this recipe from many South Indian chefs, who were proud to share this revered dish of their culinary heritage and help us understand the regional nuances of this delicious curry. After returning to Canada, we started cooking this dish and created our own version, sharing our heavenly Keralan cooking experiences with others and making sure to tout this as one of the best curries that South Indian cuisine has to offer.

PREP TIME: 30 MINUTES

COOK TIME: 25 MINUTES

YIELD: SERVES 4

1 cup coarsely chopped fresh coconut or ½ cup dried desiccated coconut, unsweetened

1 teaspoon cumin seeds

½ teaspoon mustard seeds

5 cups (or 1.1 pounds) mixed vegetables (such as bottle gourd, cauliflower, green beans, pumpkin, carrot, sweet potatoes, zucchini, or red, orange, or yellow bell peppers), cut into bite-sized pieces

1 cup water, plus extra if necessary

1 medium onion, finely sliced

8 to 10 fresh curry leaves

2 to 3 small green chilies, sliced lengthwise

1½ teaspoons sea salt, or to taste

1 teaspoon turmeric powder

½ cup dahi or Balkan-style yogurt

½ cup coconut milk

1 tablespoon coconut oil

1 | In a mortar and pestle or food processor, combine the fresh coconut and cumin seeds and mustard seeds. Coarsely grind or mince and set aside.

2 | In a medium heavy-bottomed pot, combine the mixed vegetables, water, onions, curry leaves, green chilies, salt, and turmeric. Cover and cook on medium heat for 15 minutes or until the vegetables are tender.

3 | Reduce the heat to low and add the coconut mixture, stirring to combine. Cook on low heat for another 5 minutes.

4 | In a small or medium bowl, whisk together the dahi and coconut milk until smooth, then fold this mixture into the vegetables. Add the coconut oil and thin out the mixture with extra water, if desired. Stir and simmer for another 5 minutes.

5 | Remove from the heat and serve with piping-hot plain boiled rice.

NOTE: In the fall, try this recipe using root vegetables such as butternut squash, carrots, potatoes, and pumpkin. Use similarly textured vegetables so they cook within the same time.

EGGPLANT RAVAIYA

Several years ago, my brother, Paresh, and I visited each of the villages and towns where our maternal and paternal grandparents grew up, and met relatives who lovingly embraced us as close family. On our journey through the Gujarati countryside, we stopped at a restaurant that only serves one dish—eggplant ravaiya served on a banana leaf. It's a dish that can be served on a vegetarian thali for a special occasion or simply with plain boiled rice and chapatis.

PREP TIME: 30 MINUTES

COOK TIME: 1 HOUR

YIELD: SERVES 4

8 round Indian eggplants, with stems

2 medium Russet potatoes, peeled and cut into large chunks

½ teaspoon sea salt

¼ cup sunflower oil

EGGPLANT FILLING

1 cup finely chopped onions

1 medium tomato, finely chopped

1¼ teaspoons sea salt, plus extra to taste

1 teaspoon coriander powder

1 teaspoon cumin powder

½ teaspoon Indian chili powder

½ teaspoon Warming Garam Masala (page 45)

½ teaspoon raw cane sugar

¼ teaspoon turmeric powder

¼ cup dried desiccated coconut, unsweetened, or finely grated or minced fresh coconut

2 tablespoons finely ground raw peanuts, plus extra whole peanuts for garnish

2 tablespoons finely chopped fresh cilantro , plus extra leaves for garnish

1 teaspoon freshly squeezed lemon juice

1 | Rinse and dry the eggplants. Hold an eggplant by the stem and make two cuts (a crosscut) vertically through the eggplant, halfway through, leaving the stems intact. This will create a space to place the filling. Continue with the remaining eggplants.

2 | **FOR THE EGGPLANT FILLING:** In a medium bowl, mix the onions, tomatoes, salt, coriander, cumin, chili powder, garam masala, sugar, and turmeric together. Stir to combine, then add the coconut, peanuts, cilantro, and lemon juice. Taste the filling and add salt, if required. Mix well and stuff the filling into the eggplants.

3 | In the same mixing bowl, toss the potatoes with any remaining masala. Sprinkle in ½ teaspoon salt, coating the potatoes well.

4 | In a large non-stick pot or skillet, add the oil and gently arrange the stuffed eggplants on the bottom in a single layer. Add the potatoes. Cover with a lid and cook on medium-low heat until the eggplants are soft and the potatoes are cooked, occasionally turning the eggplants over. This can take 45 minutes to 1 hour. Sprinkle with a pinch of salt to taste, if required. Garnish with extra whole peanuts and cilantro leaves. Serve as a main course with Indian flatbreads.

KERALA-STYLE COCONUT THORAN

A specialty of Keralan cooking, *thoran means a dry stir-fried vegetable dish. Memories of this simple, delicious coconut green-bean dish take me back to Kumily in the Cardamom Hills of the Western Ghats in Kerala. Beautiful, lush with emerald-green foliage, tranquil, and natural, this place is paradise. The heady and strong aromas of toasted coconut filled the morning air as food was prepared for the traditional vegetarian Keralan lunch known as sadhya (Malayalam for "feast"). With my mother and our longtime cooking-class students, Barbara, Wendy, and Susan, we explored this enchanting region, learning the traditional ways of cooking Keralan cuisine from local chefs. It was here that I learned how to cook this easy, tasty, coconutty green-bean stir-fry.*

PREP TIME: 20 MINUTES

COOK TIME: 20 MINUTES

YIELD: SERVES 4

½ pound green beans

2 tablespoons coconut oil

1 teaspoon brown mustard seeds

8 to 10 fresh curry leaves

½ cup finely chopped onions

¾ teaspoon sea salt, or to taste

1 teaspoon turmeric powder

1 teaspoon garlic paste

1 teaspoon finely shredded gingerroot

1 teaspoon finely chopped small green chilies, or to taste

½ cup water

1 cup finely grated or minced fresh coconut or dried desiccated coconut, unsweetened

1 | Cut the green beans in half, then slice them lengthwise. Set aside.

2 | In a wok or medium non-stick pot on medium-high heat, heat the oil, then add the mustard seeds. Fry for 15 to 30 seconds or until the mustard seeds begin to pop, then add the curry leaves and fry until they glisten in the oil. Add the onions and stir-fry for a few minutes, until translucent. Add the salt, turmeric, garlic paste, ginger, and green chilies and stir to combine.

3 | Lower the heat to medium-low and add the green beans. Mix and cook for 1 minute. Add the water and reduce the heat to medium. Cover with a lid and cook for 5 to 7 minutes.

4 | Remove the lid and add the coconut, stir-frying for 5 to 7 minutes or until the water is absorbed. Check that the green beans are tender. Serve with a South Indian meal as a side dish.

NOTE: We like the look of the green beans sliced lengthwise, although it takes a bit of extra time. If you're pinched for time or are looking for a variation on this recipe, you could chop the green beans into small pieces instead. A finely chopped carrot can be mixed with the green beans for yet another variation.

CAULIFLOWER & MIXED VEGETABLES WITH CRISPY OKRA

When my mother was in her teens, she woke up every morning at five o'clock to prepare a healthy lunch for her grandfather, who wasn't able to prepare his own meals. She often cooked this curry for her grandfather before departing for her two long bus rides to get to school, and it's a recipe she still cooks today. For this recipe, you can be a bit flexible with the choice of vegetables and use whatever you have in your refrigerator, but the cauliflower is a must!

PREP TIME: 15 MINUTES

COOK TIME: 35 MINUTES

YIELD: SERVES 4

2 tablespoons sunflower oil

½ teaspoon brown mustard seeds

¼ teaspoon cumin seeds

2 dried red chilies

Pinch of asafoetida

1 large tomato, finely cubed

2 cups cauliflower florets

1 medium Russet potato, peeled and cubed

1 small sweet potato, peeled and cubed

1 small zucchini, cubed

1 cup peas

2 teaspoons coriander powder

1¼ teaspoons sea salt

½ teaspoon cumin powder

½ teaspoon turmeric powder

¼ teaspoon Indian chili powder

1 teaspoon garlic paste

1 cup water

Fresh cilantro, to garnish

CRISPY OKRA GARNISH

6 fresh baby okras

1 tablespoon sunflower oil

Pinch of coriander powder

Pinch of Kashmiri chili powder

Pinch of sea salt

Pinch of turmeric powder

1 | In a medium heavy-bottomed pot, over medium-high heat, heat the oil. Add the mustard seeds and the cumin seeds and fry for 15 to 30 seconds, until the mustard seeds begin to pop. Add the dried chilies and asafoetida.

2 | Lower the heat to medium. Add the tomatoes and stir. Add the cauliflower, potatoes, sweet potatoes, zucchini, and peas. Sprinkle in the coriander, salt, cumin, turmeric, and Indian chili powder. Add the garlic paste. Mix to coat the vegetables with the spices. Cover and cook for 5 minutes.

3 | Add the water, cover, and cook on medium-low heat until the cauliflower and potatoes are softened, about 10 to 15 minutes. This mixed vegetable curry should have a thick sauce.

4 | **FOR THE CRISPY OKRA GARNISH:** Wipe the okras with a damp paper towel and slice them into rounds. Pat them with a dry paper towel to absorb any excess moisture. In a medium skillet over medium-high heat, heat the oil and add the okra, then sprinkle in the coriander, Kashmiri chili powder, salt, and turmeric. Stir-fry for up to 10 minutes or until the okra becomes crispy and golden.

5 | Sprinkle the crispy okra garnish on top of the mixed vegetables before serving. Garnish with cilantro to taste.

8

| PANEER

Creamy and bright white, paneer has a distinctive quality: it does not melt when cooked or grilled, so paneer cubes can be simmered into curry sauces or baked in a tandoor clay oven. The tradition of making cheese from cow's milk is prevalent in India, namely in the states of Punjab, where dairy cows reside in vast numbers, and also in the regions of Gujarat and West Bengal, among others. Making paneer at home is easy; it can be used as a vegetarian substitute in most non-vegetarian recipes. And because it's neutral in taste, paneer takes on Indian spices beautifully, whether it's grilled or in a curry.

HOMEMADE FRESH PANEER

Good paneer has a creamy, smooth, firm texture, a farm-fresh cheese taste, and a rich, melt-in-your-mouth quality. Making paneer at home is simple and requires only a couple of ingredients and utensils—milk, a mild acid, a colander, and a pot, plus some cheesecloth. For the milk, choose whole, as full-fat milk will give you the right texture and add full body to your paneer.

With paneer, the possibilities are endless, and it's a great vegetarian substitute for chicken or meat. Once you've tried making paneer, you'll find many ways to enjoy this homemade cheese in all your Indian curries. Try making the recipes found in the Non-Vegetarian Curries & Mains chapter using paneer as a vegetarian substitute, especially in vindaloo, korma, makhani, tikka masala, hariyali, and South Indian coconut curry.

PREP TIME: OVERNIGHT DRAINING

COOK TIME: 15 MINUTES

YIELD: ABOUT 14 OUNCES

10⅔ cups whole milk
⅓ cup white vinegar

1 | Line a colander or strainer with cheesecloth and set it in the sink.

2 | In a medium pot, bring the milk to a gentle boil. As soon as the milk starts to form a lot of little bubbles, quickly remove the pot from the heat.

3 | Add the vinegar and stir with a slotted spoon until the milk curdles into small globules and the water separates.

4 | Pour the curdled milk into the cheesecloth and gently rinse the curds with a quick run of cold water. The curds may still contain hot water, so you may want to wear gloves for the next step. Tightly twist the cheesecloth to drain out the excess liquid, then suspend the paneer ball over the sink for 1 hour to further drain.

5 | Take the paneer ball and flatten it to form a square or patty (the cheesecloth should still be wrapped around the paneer) and place it inside the colander. Place a plate or bowl under the colander to catch excess liquid, then put a weight (such as a stone mortar or a heavy pot) on the paneer "patty" and allow excess liquid to drain out in the refrigerator overnight. Note that the edges of the paneer (or anywhere the weight is not directly applied to the paneer) will be a little crumbly, so it's important to find a weight that will apply equal pressure to all parts of the paneer.

6 | Gently remove the cheesecloth and prepare the paneer as needed for a curry or dish. Paneer will keep in the refrigerator in an airtight container for up to 4 days.

SHAHI PANEER WITH SHREDDED GINGER

A dish with Moghul roots, *shahi paneer is a creamy, rich, and decadent paneer curry that's fit for a king, literally—the word shah means "king" or "ruler" in Persian, and shahi means "royalty." My first encounter with shahi paneer was at the famous Copper Chimney restaurant in the Worli district of Mumbai, accompanied by my aunty—a family friend who lives just steps away from the restaurant and was my gracious guide while I was traveling through this vibrant city. She recommended the shahi paneer off the menu as the best vegetarian option, and it arrived at the table in an opulent, bright copper balti dish. We savoured each bite, dipping into the mildly creamy sauce with hot, pillowy, freshly baked rotis topped with decadent ghee, making this one of the most memorable meals I've had in Mumbai.*

PREP TIME: 15 MINUTES

COOK TIME: 40 MINUTES

YIELD: SERVES 4

12 ounces paneer (page 154 or store-bought)

5 medium onions, peeled and coarsely cut

1⅓ cups water

½ teaspoon fennel seeds

½ teaspoon black peppercorns

1 teaspoon coriander powder

½ teaspoon cumin powder

½ teaspoon turmeric powder

¼ teaspoon Kashmiri chili powder

1 cup half-and-half cream

¼ teaspoon saffron

3 tablespoons sunflower oil

2 cinnamon sticks

2 star anise

2 bay leaves

2 whole mace pieces

½ cup unsalted crushed tomatoes

1¼ teaspoons sea salt

1 teaspoon raw cane sugar

1 teaspoon garlic paste

2 teaspoons finely shredded gingerroot

1 | Cut the paneer into ½-inch thick triangles and set aside—it's this shape that identifies this curry as shahi paneer.

2 | In a small pot, place the onions and water. Partially cover the pot, bring to a boil, and cook for 5 to 7 minutes or until the onions are softened. Drain the onions, reserving the liquid onion stock. In a food processor or blender, puree the onions until smooth.

3 | Heat a medium skillet on medium-high heat. Add the fennel seeds and peppercorns to dry-roast them. Gently toast the spices for 2 to 3 minutes, then remove the spices from the skillet to allow them to cool. Using a mortar and pestle, grind the spices into a fine powder. Mix in the coriander, cumin, turmeric, and chili powder. Set aside.

4 | In a small bowl or measuring cup, combine the cream and saffron; then set aside.

5 | In a medium non-stick pot on medium-high heat, heat the oil. Add the cinnamon and star anise and fry for 30 seconds or until the spices become fragrant. Add the bay leaves and mace and fry until fragrant, then add the pureed onions. Cook for about 15 minutes, stirring, until the onions are reduced and become slightly brown. Reduce the heat to medium-low, add the tomatoes, salt, sugar, and garlic paste, and stir to combine. Sprinkle in the prepared spice mixture from the mortar and pestle.

(continued)

Warming Garam Masala (page 15),
to garnish
Fresh cilantro, to garnish

8 | Stir in the reserved liquid onion stock and mix well. Add the cream with saffron, then gently add the paneer triangles, coating with the sauce, and simmer for a few minutes. Sprinkle the ginger over top. Garnish with garam masala and cilantro to taste.

NOTE: The best flatbread option for shahi paneer is Flaky Paranthas (page 208), as they can handle the body and thickness of this curry sauce. You can also serve this with plain boiled rice. If you love ginger, you can either add up to 1 tablespoon shredded gingerroot or gingerroot cut into matchsticks. Swirl on table cream or whipping cream just before serving to add an extra layer of decadence.

TANDOORI-SPICED PANEER KEBABS WITH GRILLING VEGETABLES

This recipe is a snap to prepare—just add the Tandoori Marinade Spice Blend (page 47) to oil along with garlic and ginger and some fresh lemon juice for the easiest of marinades. Baste this on the paneer cubes along with grilling vegetables such as red peppers, zucchini, and red onions to make the most delicious, swoon-worthy vegetarian kebabs, perfect for an Indian-style barbecue or outdoor gathering.

PREP TIME: 20 MINUTES, PLUS 1 HOUR TO SOAK THE BAMBOO SKEWERS

COOK TIME: 20 MINUTES

YIELD: 6 KEBABS

6 bamboo skewers, 9 inches long

12 ounces paneer

TANDOORI MARINADE

2½ tablespoons sunflower oil

1½ tablespoons Tandoori Marinade Spice Blend (page 47)

2 teaspoons garlic paste

2 teaspoons ginger paste

1 teaspoon freshly squeezed lemon juice

¾ teaspoon sea salt

VEGETABLES

1 medium zucchini, cut lengthwise, then thickly sliced

12 cherry tomatoes

1 medium red onion, cubed

Minty Green Cilantro Chutney (page 53), for serving

Basic Cooling Cucumber Raita (page 60), for serving

1 | In a shallow dish, soak the bamboo skewers in water for at least 1 hour to prevent them from burning.

2 | Line a baking sheet with aluminum foil. Set aside.

3 | Carefully cut the paneer into 1-inch cubes, being gentle to avoid breakage. You should get 18 pieces. Set aside.

4 | **FOR THE TANDOORI MARINADE:** In a medium bowl, mix the marinade ingredients together. Add the paneer, coating each cube well. Add the zucchini and cherry tomatoes and toss with the marinade.

5 | Set one oven rack at the top position and the other at the center position. Preheat the oven to 400°F.

6 | Gently thread three paneer cubes per bamboo skewer, alternating with zucchini cubes, cherry tomatoes, and onion cubes. Arrange the paneer kebabs on the lined baking sheet and baste with any remaining marinade.

7 | Bake in the center of the oven for 12 to 15 minutes, turning occasionally so they cook on all sides. Change the oven temperature to the broiler setting and move the baking sheet to the top oven rack. Broil for 1 to 2 minutes to give the paneer a slight char. Flip and repeat on the other side, if desired. Serve with mint cilantro chutney and cucumber raita.

| NOTE: These skewers are also fantastic cooked on a barbecue!

9

NON-VEGETARIAN CURRIES & MAINS

Many variables are considered when cooking a non-vegetarian Indian curry from scratch—spice combinations, whole spices versus ground, onion-to-tomato ratios, protein choices, freshness of ingredients, and simmer times—with each affecting the end result. This chapter features some of our cooking-class favorites and encourages you to explore different curry styles from the various regions of India. These famous non-vegetarian curries each have their own distinctive quality, whether it's a specific ingredient or style of cooking, and each tells a story, making these recipes not only delicious to indulge in but also fascinating to understand.

MURGH MAKHANI

Murgh makhani, better known as butter chicken, is one of the world's most beloved Indian curries. Over the years, I tried many times to remove our Rich & Creamy Butter Chicken cooking class from our schedule with the intention of offering our students a more diverse range of curries from India. However, whenever I removed it, messages would arrive in droves inquiring as to when our next butter chicken class was scheduled for. After seeing all these responses, we decided that this class would always be featured as one of Arvinda's signature cooking classes, as it really is so many people's favorite Indian curry to cook—and to eat! You'll notice that butter is absent from this recipe, as it's already decadent with the use of cream, but feel free to add a pat if your heart desires.

PREP TIME: 25 MINUTES, PLUS OVERNIGHT MARINATING

COOK TIME: 55 MINUTES

YIELD: SERVES 2 TO 4

MARINADE

¼ cup Balkan-style yogurt

½ teaspoon coriander powder

½ teaspoon sea salt

¼ teaspoon cumin powder

¼ teaspoon turmeric powder

¼ teaspoon Indian chili powder

1 teaspoon freshly squeezed lemon juice

1 teaspoon garlic paste

½ teaspoon ginger paste

1 pound skinless, boneless chicken breasts, cubed

1 | **FOR THE MARINADE:** In a large bowl, mix the marinade ingredients together.

2 | Add the chicken, coating it well. Cover and refrigerate the chicken overnight to marinate.

3 | Preheat the oven to 400°F and line a baking sheet with aluminum foil.

4 | Place the chicken on the baking sheet and bake for 10 minutes or until the chicken has lost its pinkness and is cooked. Set aside.

(continued)

SAUCE

5 medium onions, peeled and coarsely cut

1⅓ cups water, plus extra if necessary

2 tablespoons sunflower oil

3 black peppercorns

3 cinnamon sticks

3 green cardamom pods

3 star anise

3 whole cloves

½ cup unsalted crushed tomatoes

1 teaspoon coriander powder

½ teaspoon cumin powder

½ teaspoon turmeric powder

¼ teaspoon Indian chili powder

¾ cup half-and-half cream

2 teaspoons to 1 tablespoon raw cane sugar, to taste

¾ teaspoon sea salt, or to taste

1 teaspoon garlic paste

1 teaspoon ginger paste

Warming Garam Masala (page 45), to garnish

Fresh cilantro, finely chopped, to garnish

5 | **FOR THE SAUCE:** In a medium pot, combine the onions and 1⅓ cups water. Partially cover the pot, bring to a boil, and cook for 5 to 7 minutes, until the onions are softened. Drain the onions, reserving the liquid onion stock. In a food processor or blender, puree the onions until smooth. Set aside.

6 | In a medium non-stick pot on medium-high heat, heat the oil. Add the peppercorns, cinnamon, cardamom, star anise, and cloves. Fry for 30 seconds, until the spices become fragrant and the cardamom pods swell. Add the pureed onions and cook for 15 minutes, stirring, until the onions are reduced and become slightly brown.

7 | Reduce the heat to medium and add the tomatoes. Mix to combine, then sprinkle in the coriander, cumin, turmeric, and chili powder. Stir to mix in the spices, then add the cream, sugar, and salt and mix to combine. Simmer for a couple of minutes. Add the garlic and ginger pastes and mix into the sauce.

8 | Stir in the reserved liquid onion stock, then add the cooked chicken to the sauce. Gently coat the chicken with the sauce. Reduce the heat to medium-low, cover, and simmer for 10 minutes.

9 | Remove the lid. If needed, add water to the sauce to reach the desired consistency, and add salt to taste. Cook for a few more minutes. Garnish with garam masala and cilantro to taste. Serve with basmati rice and Whole Wheat Garlic Sesame Naan (page 206).

NOTE: When butter chicken is prepared in restaurants, it's most often cooked with tandoori chicken pieces. To get that smoky flavor, grill the marinated chicken on the barbecue and then add it to the sauce.

GOAN PORK VINDALOO

The mere mention of the word vindaloo *always takes me back to my time in Goa, the small Indian state situated in the south, with its tropical coastline, unique architecture, Bohemian towns and villages, beachfront resorts, and welcoming and relaxing vibe . . . literally the stuff of dreams! And no other curry best embodies the cuisine of Goa than vindaloo. Born from the culinary traditions of Portuguese settlers, vindaloo is a dish deep-rooted in India's recent past and is a classic example of how two unique and distinct cuisines come together to make something absolutely mouthwatering. Derived from a Portuguese dish called carne de vinho e alhos—meat cooked in wine, vinegar and garlic—the dish evolved in India to include tamarind, black pepper, and garam masala. Up until the Portuguese arrival in India in the late 15th century, black pepper was the main spice that added heat to Indian cuisine, but this all changed when the Portuguese introduced chili peppers and other New World crops for trading and cultivation, one of the reasons why red chilies are characteristic of vindaloo.*

PREP TIME: 20 MINUTES

COOK TIME: 55 MINUTES

YIELD: SERVES 2 TO 4

2 tablespoons sunflower oil

6 black peppercorns

4 green cardamom pods

3 cinnamon sticks

3 star anise

3 whole cloves

1½ cups finely chopped onions

¼ cup unsalted crushed tomatoes

2 teaspoons coriander powder

1½ teaspoons cumin powder

1¼ teaspoons Indian chili powder, plus extra if you prefer more heat

2½ teaspoons raw cane sugar

1 teaspoon sea salt, or to taste

1½ teaspoons garlic paste

1 teaspoon ginger paste

1 teaspoon concentrated tamarind paste

1 | In a medium non-stick pot on medium-high heat, heat the oil. Add the peppercorns, cardamom, cinnamon, star anise, and cloves. Fry for 30 seconds or until the spices become fragrant and the cardamom pods swell.

2 | Add the onions and fry until caramelized, stirring, for about 15 minutes. Reduce the heat to medium, add the tomatoes, and stir. Sprinkle in the coriander, cumin, and chili powder. Mix to combine. Add the sugar and salt and mix. Then add the garlic, ginger, and tamarind pastes and stir to combine.

3 | Add the pork and coat with the masala paste, stirring for 2 to 3 minutes. Cover with a lid and reduce the heat to low. Cook until the meat is tender, 10 to 15 minutes.

4 | Remove the lid, adjust the heat to medium, add the ½ cup water and vinegar, and stir. Cover and simmer for 10 minutes, giving it an occasional stir.

(continued)

1 pound boneless pork loin, cubed

½ cup water, plus extra if necessary

1 tablespoon red wine vinegar

Warming Garam Masala (page 45),
to garnish

TEMPERING INGREDIENTS

1 tablespoon sunflower oil

12 fresh curry leaves

3 to 5 small green chilies, sliced
lengthwise

5 | FOR THE TEMPERING INGREDIENTS: In a separate small non-stick pan on medium-high heat, heat the oil. Add the curry leaves and green chilies and fry for 15 seconds or until they glisten from the oil. The mixture should be sizzling hot.

6 | Pour the tempering mixture into the vindaloo and simmer for a few more minutes or until the meat is tender. Add a little water to get the desired consistency and add salt, if required.

7 | Transfer the vindaloo to a serving dish and sprinkle on garam masala to garnish. Serve this curry with Basic Boiled Fluffy Rice (page 214) and an Indian salad.

NOTE: Tamarind is an essential ingredient in this recipe. If you can't find concentrated tamarind paste, you can use 2 tablespoons tamarind pulp as a substitute.

CHICKEN TIKKA MASALA

It may surprise you to learn that chicken tikka masala is not a traditional curry with Indian roots. Some say it's from Scotland or England. Although the origins of this famous tomato-based cream curry are unclear, legend has it that a patron at an Indian restaurant ordered chicken tikka but sent it back to the kitchen because it was too dry. The South Asian chef added a can of tomato soup and a little cream on the spot to make a quick curry sauce, and the rest is history! Chicken tikka masala's impact on the British food landscape is so profound that it was declared the U.K.'s national dish in 2001, supplanting British icons such as fish and chips, Cornish pasty, and Yorkshire pudding. The celebration of chicken tikka masala in the U.K. is a wonderful example of how foods and flavors migrate and become popularized around the world as palates become increasingly international.

PREP TIME: 20 MINUTES, PLUS OVERNIGHT MARINATING

COOK TIME: 55 MINUTES

YIELD: SERVES 2 TO 4

MARINADE

¼ cup Balkan-style yogurt

1 teaspoon freshly squeezed lemon juice

1 teaspoon garlic paste

1 teaspoon ginger paste

1 teaspoon coriander powder

¾ teaspoon Warming Garam Masala (page 45)

½ teaspoon cumin powder

½ teaspoon sea salt

¼ teaspoon turmeric powder

¼ teaspoon Indian chili powder

1 pound skinless, boneless chicken breasts, cut into small chunks

1 | **FOR THE MARINADE:** In a large bowl, mix the marinade ingredients together.

2 | Add the chicken, coating it well. Cover and refrigerate the chicken overnight to marinate.

3 | Preheat the oven to 400°F and line a baking sheet with aluminum foil.

4 | Place the chicken on the baking sheet and bake for 10 minutes or until the chicken is cooked and has lost its pinkness. Set aside.

(continued)

SAUCE

5 medium onions, peeled and coarsely cut

1½ cups water, plus ½ cup if necessary

3 tablespoons sunflower oil

5 black peppercorns

4 green cardamom pods

3 cinnamon sticks

3 star anise

2 whole cloves

3 bay leaves

2 whole mace pieces

¾ cup unsalted crushed tomatoes

1 teaspoon coriander powder

1 teaspoon cumin powder

½ teaspoon Warming Garam Masala (page 45), plus extra to garnish

½ teaspoon turmeric powder

½ teaspoon Kashmiri chili powder

¼ teaspoon Indian chili powder

1 teaspoon sea salt, or to taste

¾ teaspoon raw cane sugar

1 teaspoon garlic paste

1 teaspoon ginger paste

½ cup half-and-half cream

1½ teaspoons kasoori methi (dried fenugreek leaves)

1 teaspoon freshly squeezed lemon juice

Fresh cilantro, to garnish

5 | **FOR THE SAUCE:** In a medium pot, place the onions and 1½ cups water. Partially cover the pot, bring to a boil, and cook for 5 to 7 minutes, until the onions are softened. Drain the onions, reserving the liquid onion stock for later. In a food processor or blender, puree the onions until smooth. Set aside.

6 | In a separate medium non-stick pot on medium-high heat, heat the oil. Add the peppercorns, cardamom, cinnamon, star anise, and cloves. Fry for 30 seconds, until the spices sizzle and become fragrant and the cardamom swells. Add the bay leaves and mace and fry for a few seconds. Add the pureed onions. Cook for about 15 minutes, stirring, until the onions are reduced and become slightly brown. Reduce the heat to medium, then add the tomatoes and mix to combine.

7 | Sprinkle in the coriander, cumin, garam masala, turmeric, Kashmiri chili powder, and Indian chili powder. Mix to combine, then stir in the salt and sugar. Add the garlic and ginger pastes and stir, cooking for 2 to 3 minutes to make a thick paste. Stir in the cream and the reserved liquid onion stock, then add the cooked chicken to the sauce. Cover with a lid and simmer for 10 minutes.

8 | Add the kasoori methi and lemon juice, stir, and cook for a few more minutes. Add up to ½ cup water to thin out the sauce if necessary to get the desired consistency, and add more salt if required. Garnish with garam masala and cilantro to taste. Serve with basmati rice, Whole Wheat Garlic Sesame Naan (page 206), and a vegetable curry to make a full meal.

FRAGRANT SOUTH INDIAN COCONUT SHRIMP WITH CURRY LEAVES

On one of our culinary trips to India, my mother and I were strolling on a beach in Kerala on a sun-drenched afternoon when two young men handed us a flyer for their beach restaurant called Fish & Chips, which happened to be located exactly where we were standing (though there were no tables, chairs, or a kitchen in sight, and the menu wasn't offering any fish or chips!). Nevertheless, we were won over by their enthusiasm and decided to try the restaurant for dinner. When we arrived at the same spot at dinnertime, the dark beach was lit only by the moon. Out of seemingly nowhere, we were met with a flashlight beam, then escorted to a table beautifully set with a white tablecloth, candles, banana leaves, and flowers. Soon the dishes we ordered started filing out to our table, and this Keralan coconut curry was one of them. It was coconutty and deliciously prepared with extra-jumbo local prawns caught just hours before. The sauce was a touch sweet from the coconut milk, but balanced by the fresh curry leaves and some chili heat. It was undoubtedly one of the best meals we've ever had in India. For this recipe, we're using shrimp but you can also make it with prawns.

PREP TIME: 10 MINUTES

COOK TIME: 30 MINUTES

YIELD: SERVES 2 TO 4

2 tablespoons coconut oil

½ teaspoon brown mustard seeds

10 fresh curry leaves

1 to 2 dried red chilies, to taste

1 large onion, finely sliced

2 medium ripe tomatoes, chopped

1 teaspoon coriander powder

1 teaspoon sea salt, or to taste

¾ teaspoon cumin powder

½ teaspoon Indian chili powder

½ teaspoon turmeric powder

¼ teaspoon raw cane sugar

½ teaspoon garlic paste

½ teaspoon ginger paste

1 cup coconut milk

1 | In a medium non-stick pot on medium-high heat, heat the oil. Add the mustard seeds and fry for 30 seconds or until they begin to pop. Add the curry leaves and dried chilies and fry for a few seconds, until they glisten. Add the onions and fry until caramelized and golden brown, about 15 minutes, stirring to ensure they don't burn.

2 | Reduce the heat to medium, add the tomatoes, and cook for a couple of minutes. Sprinkle in the coriander, salt, cumin, chili powder, turmeric, and sugar. Stir to combine, then add the garlic and ginger pastes. Fry for a couple of minutes, until the ingredients are blended into a masala.

3 | Stir in the coconut milk and gently simmer for a few minutes to make a thick sauce. Add the coconut and at least ¼ cup water to get the desired sauce consistency.

4 | Add the shrimp and cook for 5 minutes or until they are just cooked and have turned pink. Take care not to overcook the shrimp.

(continued)

¼ cup finely grated or minced fresh coconut or dried desiccated coconut, unsweetened

¼ cup water, plus extra if necessary

1 pound large shrimp (fresh or frozen and thawed), shelled and deveined

Fresh cilantro, to garnish

5 | Transfer to a serving dish and garnish with cilantro to taste. Serve hot with Basic Boiled Fluffy Rice (page 214) and an Indian salad.

NOTE: As a variation, this recipe can also be made with boneless white fish pieces, such as wild-caught haddock, known for its meaty and flaky texture, which takes the coconut curry flavors so nicely. Alternatively, this curry can easily be made vegan, as the sauce itself is vegan. Add chickpeas, sweet potatoes or squash, tempeh or tofu, or cauliflower florets!

SUCCULENT TANDOORI CHICKEN

When my brother and I were younger, my mother surprised us all by bringing home our very own tandoor oven, handcrafted in India. We were so excited to get it fired up to start cooking. But where was the user guide? The only advice given was to season or cure the clay before the first use, and from there we were on our own! After much research, trial and error, experimentation, and a lot of patience, we finally got it right, and wow, does it ever deliver once you understand the art of cooking with a tandoor. A labor of love over a few hours on a lazy, hazy summer afternoon, cooking in a traditional tandoor oven results in absolutely astounding succulence and depth of flavor like no other roasting style. Tandoori chicken is the king of the tandoor and is one of India's most beloved foods, enjoyed around the world. But no tandoor oven, no problem. Over the years, we have refined our oven-baked method, which we're sharing in this recipe (though you can also cook this on a regular barbecue, too!). When creating a tandoori barbecue menu, take care to keep lots of different chutneys on hand, including Minty Green Cilantro Chutney (page 53) and Sweet & Tangy Tamarind Date Chutney (page 54), as well as raita and kachumber to serve on the side.

PREP TIME: 30 MINUTES, PLUS 4 HOURS TO OVERNIGHT MARINATING

COOK TIME: 35 MINUTES

YIELD: SERVES 4

2½ pounds skinless, bone-in chicken pieces (10 thighs or legs)

4 lemon wedges, to garnish

Fresh cilantro, to garnish

MARINADE

½ cup Balkan-style yogurt

2 tablespoons Tandoori Marinade Spice Blend (page 47)

2 tablespoons sunflower oil

1 tablespoon freshly squeezed lemon juice

1½ tablespoons garlic paste

1 tablespoon ginger paste

2 teaspoons sea salt, or to taste

1 teaspoon Warming Garam Masala (page 45)

1 | Using a sharp knife, score the chicken pieces so the marinade will penetrate through.

2 | **FOR THE MARINADE:** In a large bowl, combine the marinade ingredients. Add the chicken and coat evenly. Cover the bowl, refrigerate, and marinate overnight or for at least 4 hours.

3 | Line a baking sheet with aluminum foil. Set one oven rack at the top position and the other at the center position. Preheat the oven to 400°F.

4 | Place the marinated chicken on the baking sheet and bake in the center of the oven for 20 minutes. Flip the chicken over and return it to the oven for another 10 minutes or until the chicken is fully cooked. Change the oven temperature to the broiler setting and move the baking sheet to the top oven rack. Broil the chicken for 2 minutes to give it a slight char. Flip and repeat on the other side, if desired.

5 | Garnish with lemon wedges and cilantro to taste. Serve with Minty Green Cilantro Chutney (page 53), Sweet & Tangy Tamarind Date Chutney (page 54), and Basic Cooling Cucumber Raita (page 60).

MAACHI MASALA

The story of this dish is distinctly Canadian and connects me to a memory of my childhood. When my brother and I were children, our parents rented cottages in midsummer with a dozen other families at Rice Lake, near Peterborough, Ontario. The best weekends ever, these cottage trips were filled with family, friends, fun, and, of course, so much food! Each family cooked up their own specialties, and the lunch and dinner buffets were as delicious and endless as the jokes and good laughs. One summertime activity at the cottage that got us hooked was fishing (pun intended!). Right off the dock, we caught sunfish and bluegill by the buckets, which we proudly brought back to our mother, who of course always had her masala box on hand. Dad gutted the fish and Mom marinated the fresh catch with her signature masala, ready for the evening's communal barbecue. After a quick cook on the grill and a squeeze of lemon, the masala fish was a resounding hit—freshly caught local fish and Indian spices are a perfect summertime match!

PREP TIME: 25 MINUTES,
PLUS 4 HOURS MARINATING

COOK TIME: 25 MINUTES

YIELD: SERVES 4

1½ pounds whole fish, gutted (see Note)

8 long sprigs fresh cilantro

6 lemon slices

3 tablespoons sunflower oil, for frying

Lemon slices, to garnish

Fresh cilantro, to garnish

MASALA PASTE

½ teaspoon brown mustard seeds

¼ teaspoon black peppercorns

1 tablespoon coriander powder

1½ teaspoons cumin powder

1½ teaspoons sea salt

½ teaspoon Indian chili powder

½ teaspoon turmeric powder

3 tablespoons sunflower oil

2 teaspoons garlic paste

1 teaspoon kasoori methi (dried fenugreek leaves)

1 | Using a sharp knife, score the fish exterior to allow the masala marinade to penetrate. When gutted, the fish will have a lengthwise cut along the ventral side (bottom portion at the belly). Keep the fish in the refrigerator.

2 | **FOR THE MASALA PASTE:** Heat a small skillet on medium-high heat. Add the mustard seeds and peppercorns. Cook for a couple of minutes, until the spices are fragrant. Transfer them to a mortar and pestle and allow the spices to cool slightly, then grind them into a fine powder. Mix in the coriander, cumin, salt, chili powder, and turmeric and mix until uniform.

3 | Transfer the masala mixture to a medium bowl and mix in the oil, garlic paste, and methi. Mix well to create the masala paste.

4 | Using a brush or clean hands, massage the masala paste all over the exterior of the fish and inside the cavity, coating the whole fish well. Place cilantro sprigs in the cavity. Cover and marinate the fish for 4 hours in the refrigerator.

5 | Place the lemon slices inside the fish cavity.

6 | In a large non-stick skillet on medium heat, heat the 3 tablespoons oil. Add the fish and cook for 20 to 25 minutes, gently turning occasionally to cook on both sides until slightly crispy. Garnish with lemon slices and cilantro to taste.

NOTE: Choose a sustainably caught fish of your choice. The masala used in this recipe pairs well with a variety of fish, including wild-caught salmon, lake trout, and arctic char, and can be used as a marinade for either a whole fish or filets. This recipe also works well using a barbecue.

LAMB KORMA

Korma is another famous Moghul specialty, where an onion-based curry of cream, yogurt, ground nuts, and saffron is slowly simmered so the meat is tender and cooked to perfection. You can substitute chicken for the lamb, if you like. This is a great option for those who steer clear of hot and spicy chili curries. It's mild but just as delicious. Serve korma with Kashmiri Dum Aloo (page 137) and Flaky Paranthas (page 208) to get a full North Indian culinary experience.

PREP TIME: 35 MINUTES

COOK TIME: 1 HOUR

YIELD: SERVES 2 TO 4

2 tablespoons sunflower oil

5 green cardamom pods

3 whole cloves

2 cinnamon sticks

½ teaspoon cumin seeds

4 bay leaves

1½ cups finely chopped onions

1 teaspoon coriander powder

1 teaspoon cumin powder

1 teaspoon turmeric powder

½ teaspoon Kashmiri chili powder

1 teaspoon garlic paste

1 teaspoon ginger paste

1 pound boneless leg of lamb, cut into small cubes

1¼ teaspoons sea salt, or to taste

½ cup dahi or Balkan-style yogurt, room temperature

½ cup half-and-half cream

8 to 10 saffron strands

¼ cup ground almonds or ground cashews

¼ cup water, plus extra if necessary

Warming Garam Masala (page 45), to garnish

Fresh cilantro, to garnish

1 | In a medium non-stick pot on medium-high heat, heat the oil. Add the cardamom, cloves, and cinnamon and fry for 30 seconds or until the spices become fragrant and the cardamom pods swell. Add the cumin seeds and stir, then add the bay leaves. Fry until the cumin seeds are fragrant and light golden. Add the onions and fry, stirring, until golden brown and caramelized, about 15 minutes.

2 | Reduce the heat to medium, then add the coriander, cumin powder, turmeric, and chili powder. Mix to combine. Add the garlic and ginger pastes, mix, and cook for 1 minute, until fragrant.

3 | Add the lamb and sprinkle in the salt. Gently fold the lamb into the masala paste to coat.

4 | Reduce the heat to low, cover with a lid, and cook for 15 minutes, stirring occasionally. The lamb should be cooked and tender.

5 | Meanwhile, in a medium bowl, whisk the yogurt and cream together and stir in the saffron to allow its flavor to release. Gently add the mixture to the lamb. Fold in the almonds. Cover with a lid and simmer on low heat for 15 minutes or until the meat is fully tender and cooked. Add the water to thin out the curry sauce, adding as much as required to reach the desired consistency. Add more salt if required. Stir and simmer for 5 minutes.

6 | Transfer to a serving dish and garnish with garam masala and cilantro to taste. Serve with an Indian flatbread and basmati rice.

INDIAN-STYLE KEBABS
WITH GRILLING VEGETABLES

On the last night of my whirlwind tour of India several years ago, I had the chance to enjoy a night on the town in Mumbai with some old friends. We ate our way through Mumbai, savoring multiple courses of delicious Indian foods, going from one hot spot to the next. From fine dining at a private social club, to cheap, tasty street foods, to late-night, after-club, back-alley eats, it was one amazing epicurean night in India's most glamorous city. My incredible hosts (self-proclaimed foodies themselves) pulled out all the stops to treat us to the city's finest and most famous dining experiences. At one point during the evening, we came across street stalls that were cooking up a variety of ground meat kebabs served hot off a charcoal grill. The humid night air felt electric with the latest Bollywood tunes blasting and crowds of young people milling about. For Mumbaikars, kebabs seem to be a nighttime street-food favorite. Indian kebabs include garam masala, which adds a wide variety of distinctly Indian spices and flavors, such as cardamom, cinnamon, and fennel. For a variation, this kebab meat base can be made into patties to make Indian-style burgers, topped with onion, lettuce, tomatoes, and fresh chutneys.

PREP TIME: 45 MINUTES,
PLUS 1 HOUR TO SOAK
THE BAMBOO SKEWERS

COOK TIME: 20 MINUTES

YIELD: SERVES 4

8 to 10 bamboo skewers,
9 inches long

1 pound lean ground chicken

2 teaspoons coriander powder

1½ teaspoons cumin powder

1¼ teaspoons sea salt

1 teaspoon Warming Garam
Masala (page 45)

¼ teaspoon Indian chili powder

½ cup finely chopped onions

½ cup finely chopped fresh cilantro

2 small green chilies, finely chopped

1½ teaspoons garlic paste

½ teaspoon ginger paste

1 | In a shallow dish, soak the bamboo skewers in water for at least 1 hour to prevent them from burning.

2 | In a large bowl, place the ground chicken and sprinkle in the coriander, cumin, salt, garam masala, and chili powder, distributing the spices evenly on top. Add the onions, cilantro, green chilies, and garlic and ginger pastes, and using a fork or your hands, mix together well to combine. Cover the bowl and refrigerate for 10 to 15 minutes.

3 | Set one oven rack at the top position and the other at the center position. Line a baking sheet with aluminum foil. Preheat the oven to 400°F.

4 | Thread a piece of grilling vegetable of your choice onto the bottom of a soaked skewer, taking care to leave a gap so you can pick it up. Take a small amount of ground chicken mixture (about 2 tablespoons), form an oval-shaped kebab about 3 inches long, and thread it onto the skewer. You can rub a little oil onto your hands if the chicken sticks. Add another grilling vegetable and then another kebab. Continue with the remaining chicken mixture, vegetables, and skewers until you have two kebabs per skewer, alternating with vegetables.

(continued)

1 pound skinless, boneless chicken breasts, cut into cubes

¾ cup water, plus extra if necessary

¼ cup dahi or Balkan-style yogurt

2 to 3 small green chilies, sliced lengthwise

¼ cup half-and-half cream

Whole nutmeg, finely grated, to garnish

Fresh cilantro, to garnish

5 | Stir in the cream and simmer for a couple of minutes. Add a little extra water if necessary to get the desired consistency, and adjust the salt if required. Garnish with a light dusting of freshly grated nutmeg and cilantro to taste.

NOTE: This recipe was created using our garam masala recipe (page 45). If you are using a different garam masala, the spicing of this dish will be different so adjust your spicing accordingly, as needed.

HARIYALI CHICKEN ON SKEWERS

My first encounter with the word hariyali, *the Hindi word for greenery, was when watching the 1962 Bollywood classic* Hariyali Aur Rasta, *a love story set in the beautiful, lush green hilltops of Darjeeling, West Bengal's famed tea-growing region. This grilled chicken specialty shares the same name thanks to its beautiful spinach and mint-green marinade. It's the plentiful amounts of fresh green ingredients—cilantro, mint, spinach, and fresh fenugreek leaves (methi)—that make this chicken marinade so lively, robust, and deliciously impeccable.*

PREP TIME: 45 MINUTES, PLUS OVERNIGHT MARINATING AND 1 HOUR TO SOAK THE BAMBOO SKEWERS

COOK TIME: 35 MINUTES

YIELD: SERVES 4

1½ pounds skinless, boneless chicken breasts

6 bamboo skewers, 9 inches long

4 lemon wedges, to garnish

Cilantro Mint Yogurt Drizzle (page 71), for serving

HARIYALI MARINADE

3 tablespoons sunflower oil

1½ cups loosely packed fresh mint leaves

1 cup chopped fresh cilantro

½ cup chopped spinach

½ cup chopped fresh fenugreek leaves (optional)

2 tablespoons chopped garlic chives

1 to 2 small green chilies, finely chopped, to taste

1 tablespoon garlic paste

1 tablespoon freshly squeezed lemon juice

1½ teaspoons sea salt

1 tablespoon coriander powder

1 teaspoon cumin seeds

½ teaspoon turmeric powder

1 | Cut the chicken into cubes, place them in a medium bowl, and set them aside in the refrigerator.

2 | **FOR THE HARIYALI MARINADE:** In a blender or food processor, blend all the marinade ingredients together until smooth. Add the marinade to the chicken and coat well. Cover the bowl and refrigerate to marinate overnight.

3 | In a shallow dish, soak the bamboo skewers in water for at least 1 hour to prevent them from burning. They can also be left overnight.

4 | Line a baking sheet with aluminum foil. Set one oven rack at the top position and the other at the center position. Preheat the oven to 350°F.

5 | Thread the marinated chicken pieces onto the soaked bamboo skewers.

6 | Transfer the skewers to the baking sheet and bake in the oven for 15 minutes. Flip them over to cook the chicken evenly for another 15 minutes or until the chicken has lost its pinkness and is cooked. Change the oven temperature to the broiler setting and move the baking sheet to the top oven rack. Broil the chicken for 2 minutes to give it a slight char. Flip and repeat on the other side, if desired.

7 | Garnish with lemon wedges and cilantro mint yogurt drizzle, and serve with basmati rice pullao and fresh naan.

NOTE: You can also cook the hariyali chicken on a barbecue or grill. The best vegetarian option for this delicious marinade is paneer, while tofu is a great vegan option.

MAPLED TANDOORI SALMON WITH MINT

My mother and I created this special dish for our Epicurean Indian Valentine cooking class. When putting the menu together for this class, we were mindful to choose red vegetables and spices, so any recipe using our Tandoori Marinade Spice Blend would fit in quite nicely. This recipe isn't too fussy, so it's a good one to prepare for Valentine's Day—or for a summer barbecue.

PREP TIME: 15 MINUTES,
PLUS 1 HOUR MARINATING

COOK TIME: 10 MINUTES

YIELD: SERVES 4

1 pound skinless, boneless salmon filets (about 4)

2 tablespoons olive oil, plus extra for cooking

2 tablespoons Tandoori Marinade Spice Blend (page 47)

½ teaspoon sea salt

2 tablespoons pure maple syrup

Fresh mint, to garnish

1 | In a medium bowl, place the salmon filets. In a small bowl, combine the oil, tandoori marinade spice blend, and salt and mix well. Add the marinade to the salmon, coating well on all sides. Cover the bowl and marinate in the refrigerator for at least 1 hour.

2 | Heat a large non-stick, heavy-bottomed skillet on medium-high heat and add 1 tablespoon oil. Arrange the salmon filets in the skillet and cook on one side for 5 minutes. Using a pastry brush, glaze the salmon with maple syrup. Flip and cook for another 5 minutes or until the salmon reaches your desired doneness, and glaze the top with maple syrup.

3 | Garnish the salmon with fresh mint to taste and serve with Minty Green Cilantro Chutney (page 53), Lemon Coconut Cranberry Pullao (page 227), and a vegetable side. The perfect salad pairing would be our Beet, Carrot & Cabbage Kachumber with Garam Masala Vinaigrette (page 69), as it's also a beautiful red color.

INSTANT POT KASHMIRI ROGAN JOSH

In the northernmost part of India is Jammu and Kashmir, where the most famous dish is a mutton curry called rogan josh (rogan means "ghee" and josh means "braised"), brought to this area by the Moghuls. This version of the recipe uses lamb, and the Instant Pot is the perfect way to cook it so it's tender, buttery, and falls right off the bone. The addition of saffron is special too, as this mountainous region is the primary region in India where saffron is grown and cultivated.

PREP TIME: 25 MINUTES, PLUS 10 MINUTES INSTANT POT NATURAL PRESSURE RELEASE

COOK TIME: 1 HOUR 10 MINUTES

YIELD: SERVES 2 TO 4

1 teaspoon cumin seeds

½ teaspoon fennel seeds

¼ teaspoon black peppercorns

2 pounds bone-in lamb shoulder chops, cut into pieces

1¾ teaspoons sea salt, divided, plus extra to taste

1¼ cups water, plus extra if necessary

2 tablespoons ghee

3 cinnamon sticks

3 green cardamom pods

3 whole cloves

2 bay leaves

2 dried red chilies

1 black cardamom pod

1 whole mace piece

1½ cups finely chopped onions

2 tablespoons unsalted crushed tomatoes

1½ teaspoons Kashmiri chili powder

1 teaspoon coriander powder

½ teaspoon Warming Garam Masala (page 45), plus extra to garnish

½ teaspoon turmeric powder

1 | Heat a small skillet on medium-high heat. Add the cumin seeds, fennel seeds, and black peppercorns and gently toast them for 30 seconds, stirring until the cumin seeds become fragrant and light golden. Transfer to a mortar and pestle and slightly cool, then grind the spices into a fine powder. Set aside.

2 | Add the lamb pieces to the Instant Pot in a single layer. In a measuring cup, dissolve ¾ teaspoon salt in 1¼ cups water, then pour over the lamb. Take care to secure the lid correctly and be sure the pressure release valve is set to the sealing position. This is very important. The Instant Pot will register as "on." Adjust the setting to "pressure cook high" and set the timer for 25 minutes. Once the pressure cooking is complete, the Instant Pot will begin the natural pressure release. Allow for 10 minutes of natural pressure release, then release the remaining pressure by carefully setting the pressure release valve to venting. Always wear an oven mitt or glove when venting and keep your hands and face away from the vent, as the steam is extremely hot and can burn! Handle the valve from the side, not from above. Open the lid only when it is safe to do so, checking that all the pressure has been released first. Using tongs, transfer the lamb pieces from the Instant Pot to a bowl, along with any liquid in the pot. Set aside.

3 | Adjust the Instant Pot setting to "sauté more." Melt the ghee and add the cinnamon, green cardamom, cloves, bay leaves, red chilies, black cardamom, and mace. Stir and fry the spices for 30 seconds or until the cardamom pods swell, taking care they do not burn. Reduce the setting to "sauté less," then add the onions and fry for 10 minutes, stirring until the onions become golden brown, translucent, and soft. Add the tomatoes. Sprinkle in the ground spices from the mortar and pestle and mix in.

(continued)

Pinch of asafoetida (optional)

1 teaspoon garlic paste

1 teaspoon ginger paste

½ cup dahi or Balkan-style yogurt, room temperature

8 to 10 saffron strands

Fresh cilantro, finely chopped, to garnish

4 | Sprinkle in the chili powder, coriander, remaining 1 teaspoon salt, garam masala, turmeric, and asafoetida. Mix for a minute to combine. Stir in the garlic and ginger pastes.

5 | Return the lamb to the Instant Pot along with the reserved liquid. Deglaze the bottom of the pot and stir to combine.

6 | Add the dahi and saffron. Gently fold in, then simmer for 10 minutes, stirring occasionally. Add extra water if necessary to get the desired consistency and adjust the salt if required.

7 | Garnish with garam masala and cilantro to taste. Serve with basmati rice and Whole Wheat Garlic Sesame Naan (page 206).

10
| FLATBREADS

India's "breadbasket" lies in the northern states of Punjab and Haryana, both prolific wheat-growing regions that fuel the diverse flatbread-making traditions across the country. Most Indian meals in northern and central India are accompanied by flatbreads, and they are the perfect vehicle for scooping up and enjoying a curry. Specific flatbreads pair with specific dishes, complementing textures and tastes to make the meal that much more enjoyable. These recipes will help you to delve into India's flatbread-making tradition at home.

An optional method for cooking the dry papads is to grill them using tongs on top of a gas stove or on a wire rack on an electrical stovetop. Another easy method is to microwave a single papad on high heat for about 1 minute, but do keep an eye on it, as cooking times may vary from microwave to microwave. Change up the flavor of papads by swapping out the cumin seeds for freshly cracked black pepper, finely chopped green chilies, red chili powder, red chili flakes, or, for something with less heat, garlic powder.

CUMIN-SCENTED PAPADS

When I was younger, every one of my visits to England included a visit to aunt Jaya Foi's house in Wembley. Her home was always a haven of culinary inspiration. She had the kindest heart, was a talented, passionate Indian cook, and was my mother's mentor and guardian. On one such visit, we arrived on a day when my aunt was making papads (commonly known as pappadums) with some neighbors and helpers in the backyard. Everyone was involved in the assembly line of rolling out the papads and taking them out back to dry. Once dried, the papads were stored in large stainless-steel dabbas (drums) so they would be readily available for an Indian meal. Inspired by our aunt, this recipe shares in that spirit of making papads at home from scratch. All that's really needed is finely ground lentil flour made from urad dal and time for the papads to completely dry. Lentil-based papads are gluten-free and served as part of a vegetarian thali (vegetarian meal), offering a savory crunch, texture, and excitement alongside dals, Indian vegetable dishes (referred to as sabjis), pickles, and chapatis—taking an Indian meal from fantastic to absolutely perfect!

PREP TIME: 45 MINUTES, PLUS 10 MINUTES RESTING AND OVERNIGHT DRYING

COOK TIME: 15 MINUTES

YIELD: 10 PAPADS

½ cup warm water

1 teaspoon cumin seeds

1 teaspoon sea salt

¼ teaspoon baking powder

Pinch of asafoetida

1 cup urad flour, plus extra for dusting

2 teaspoons sunflower oil, plus extra for deep-frying

1 | In a small pot, combine the water, cumin seeds, salt, baking powder, and asafoetida. Simmer on medium heat for 5 to 7 minutes. Remove from the heat and allow the mixture to cool.

2 | In a paraat or bowl, place the flour and mix in the water mixture. Combine well to make a firm dough. Add the oil and knead the dough for 5 to 10 minutes. Allow to rest, uncovered, for 10 minutes.

3 | Divide the dough into 10 evenly sized balls and roll them out into thin, circular wafers 5½ to 6 inches in diameter, using the urad flour for dusting. Lay the papads out onto two baking sheets and allow them to dry overnight. This could take longer depending on the temperature of your kitchen.

4 | Fill a kadhai, wok, or deep-fryer with oil 2 inches deep and heat it on medium-high. Test the oil temperature by dropping a little dough into the oil. If it immediately floats to the top, the oil is ready. Fry one papad at a time, cooking it until light in color. Drain the papads on paper towel and serve with a complete Indian meal.

11

| INDIAN RICE

Basmati rice is world-famous for its signature aroma, long and fine delicate grains, and beautifully fluffy quality. Cooking basmati rice with aromatic spices and ghee makes it extraordinary! Complementing both vegetarian and non-vegetarian curries and mains, piping-hot rice may arrive to the table as a second course after all the flatbreads are consumed, allowing you to go for a second helping of curry. Always serve rice fresh and hot with a garnish of cilantro and a light sprinkling of perfumy garam masala for added opulence. In this chapter, we explore different Indian rice preparations to serve with all the curries in this cookbook.

BASIC BOILED FLUFFY RICE

In Indian cuisine, rarely do you find foods of any sort, whether appetizers or drinks, curries or desserts, where spices are absent from the recipe. However, there are exceptions, and one exception is rice. When we want the spices in a particular curry to take center stage, it's best to serve it with plain boiled rice with just a pat of ghee swirled in at the top. A Goan Pork Vindaloo (page 171) that's loaded with chilies and aromatic spices is a good example, as is a tomatoey Punjabi Rajma curry (page 123) or Cauliflower & Mixed Vegetables with Crispy Okra (page 150). If basmati is not on hand, use a long-grain rice like Patna, which pairs nicely with saucy, full-bodied curries as well.

PREP TIME: 5 MINUTES, PLUS 10 MINUTES SOAKING

COOK TIME: 20 MINUTES

YIELD: SERVES 4

1 cup basmati rice

1½ cups water, plus ¼ cup extra if necessary

½ teaspoon sea salt

1 teaspoon ghee

1 | In a large bowl, rinse the rice in four to five changes of lukewarm water until the water runs relatively clear. Drain and cover with fresh lukewarm water and soak the rice for 10 minutes.

2 | Rinse the rice again in a couple more changes of lukewarm water. Drain and transfer to a medium non-stick, heavy-bottomed pan. Add 1½ cups water and the salt, cover with a lid, and bring the rice to a boil on medium-high heat.

3 | Once the water has evaporated, reduce the heat to low and test if the rice grains are cooked by taking a couple of grains of rice and pinching them between your thumb and index finger. If the rice is al dente, sprinkle in up to ¼ cup water, cover, and cook on low heat for 5 more minutes.

4 | When the rice is ready, fluff it with a fork and stir in the ghee before serving with any curry or dal.

NOTE: The purpose of rinsing the rice in several changes of water is to remove any dirt and some of the starch. Lukewarm water is favored so the grains do not break. The result is fluffy and separated rice grains!

MATTAR PULLAO

A well-made basmati rice pullao that's fluffy, aromatic, and beautifully separated is highly desirable and demonstrates an Indian cook's skill. Rice is an integral part of an Indian meal, so it is absolutely vital to get it right. No pressure! No matter how deliciously perfect the curries are, the Indian meal will not be enjoyed in the same way if the rice is too mushy, overcooked, or undercooked. This classic rice preparation with peas looks fresh and vibrant, is scented with cumin, and complements the simplest or the most elaborate of Indian curries.

PREP TIME: 5 MINUTES,
PLUS 10 MINUTES SOAKING

COOK TIME: 20 MINUTES

YIELD: SERVES 4

1 cup basmati rice

1 teaspoon ghee

½ teaspoon cumin seeds

½ cup peas

1 teaspoon sea salt

1½ cups water, plus extra if necessary

Warming Garam Masala (page 45), to garnish

Fresh cilantro, to garnish

1 | In a large bowl, rinse the rice in four to five changes of lukewarm water until the water runs relatively clear. Drain and cover with fresh lukewarm water and soak the rice for 10 minutes.

2 | Rinse the rice again in a couple more changes of lukewarm water. Drain.

3 | In a medium non-stick pan or pot on medium-high heat, melt the ghee. Add the cumin seeds and fry until they become fragrant and light golden brown.

4 | Reduce the heat to medium. Add the peas and salt and cook for 1 minute. Add the rice and, using a flat utensil, gently fold so each grain of rice is evenly coated with ghee. Be gentle with the rice at this stage, as the grains can easily break.

5 | Pour in the water, enough to just cover the grains. Cover with a lid and bring to a boil on medium-high heat, cooking until the water is completely absorbed, about 10 minutes. Do not stir. Once the water is absorbed, reduce the heat to low and check if the rice is fully cooked by taking a couple of grains and pinching them between your thumb and index finger. If the rice is still al dente, sprinkle in an extra 2 to 3 tablespoons water and gently mix it in with the rice and cook for a couple of minutes further.

6 | Remove the pan from the heat and allow the rice to stand, covered, for 5 to 10 minutes. To serve, fluff the rice with a fork and garnish with a sprinkle of garam masala and cilantro to taste.

NOTE: If you're not too fussy about the presentation, serve the rice right out of the pot, as it will keep hot for longer. A typical Indian meal usually starts off with curries and fresh, hot flatbreads. When guests take a second helping of curries, the second round is served with rice, so keeping it in the pot will ensure it stays at a good hot temperature.

SOUTH INDIAN UTTAPAMS
WITH RED ONION, GREEN CHILI & CILANTRO

In Kerala, Tamil Nadu, and other parts of India's southern regions, breakfast consists of savory foods rather than something sweet. Some of my fondest memories of South India are breakfast uttapams, which are rice-based savory pancakes. What makes them even more wonderful is the addition of the onion and cilantro, which add freshness to an early morning start.

PREP TIME: 15 MINUTES,
PLUS 2 HOURS SOAKING AND
OVERNIGHT FERMENTING

COOK TIME: 40 MINUTES

YIELD: 10 TO 12 UTTAPAMS

1 cup Patna rice, long-grain rice, or short-grain rice

½ cup split and hulled urad dal (black gram lentils)

1 cup water

1 teaspoon sea salt

1 small red onion, finely chopped

¼ cup finely chopped fresh cilantro

1 to 2 small green chilies, finely chopped, to taste

Sunflower oil, for shallow frying

1 | In two separate medium bowls, rinse the rice and the dal in two to three changes of warm water. Cover both in warm water and set aside for 2 hours to soak.

2 | Rinse the rice and lentils again in two to three changes of water or until the water runs relatively clear. Drain the rice and the lentils and place them both in a blender. Add the water and salt and blend it all into a smooth batter. The uttapam batter should be thick, like a pancake batter. Transfer the batter to a medium bowl, cover, and set aside on the countertop to ferment overnight.

3 | Stir in the onions, cilantro, and green chilies to taste.

4 | In a medium tawa or non-stick frying pan on medium-high heat, heat 1 teaspoon oil. Add ¼ cup of the batter and, with a circular motion, spread the batter to make a thick circle. Cook until golden brown on one side, about 2 minutes, then flip and cook on the other side. Transfer to a plate and continue with the remaining batter. Serve the uttapams with South Indian coconut curries, coconut chutney, and pickles.

NOTE: As the rice and lentils are whole, blend the batter well so it yields smooth uttapams.

BASIC KHICHADI

So many cuisines around the world prepare dishes of rice and beans (or lentils) because these meals are hearty, healthy, and simply delicious whole meals in one. The Indian version of this is khichadi. If you have not discovered khichadi yet, in short, it's the most comforting one-pot meal in the Indian diet. A key tenet of Ayurveda states that food is our medicine—and khichadi is our trusted remedy for when immunity is low, when we're suffering from an illness, or when we need to regain strength. Ayurveda advocates khichadi as the ultimate food for proper nourishment and to help the body rid itself of toxins (known as ama) when recovering from such ailments. When khichadi is eaten as part of a simple diet, the body is able to regain its balance. For regular healthy maintenance, we have khichadi once per week as a cleanse. Split moong dal is the most common and best lentil to use for khichadi as it's easily digestible and the green moong skins are an aesthetically pleasing contrast to the basmati rice, giving the dish its distinctive appearance of rice and lentils. For this dish and all Indian rice dishes in general, cook with a good-quality, non-stick, heavy-bottomed pot so the rice does not stick to the pan.

PREP TIME: 5 MINUTES,
PLUS 1 HOUR SOAKING

COOK TIME: 20 MINUTES

YIELD: SERVES 4 TO 6

1 cup basmati rice or long-grain rice

½ cup moong dal (split), dried

1 tablespoon ghee, plus extra
to garnish

1 teaspoon sea salt, or to taste

½ teaspoon turmeric powder

3 cups water, plus extra if necessary

1 | In two separate medium bowls, rinse the rice and the dal in two to three changes of lukewarm water. Cover the rice in lukewarm water and set aside to soak for 10 minutes. Cover the dal in warm water and set aside to soak for 1 hour.

2 | Rinse the rice and lentils again in two to three changes of lukewarm water. Drain and set aside. In a medium non-stick pan or pot on medium-high heat, melt the ghee. Add the drained rice and lentils and, using a flat utensil, gently fold so each grain of rice is evenly coated with ghee. Sprinkle in the salt and turmeric and add the 3 cups water.

3 | Partially cover and cook on medium heat until all the water is absorbed and the lentils and rice are cooked, 10 to 15 minutes. Fluff with a fork and garnish with a pat of ghee on top. Serve hot with curries.

VEGETABLE BIRYANI WITH SAFFRON & NUTS

Biryani, an opulent Indian layered rice dish with origins in Persia, is a glorious preparation of saffron and cardamom-scented basmati rice baked with seasoned mixed vegetables or marinated meat, jeweled with rich dried fruits and nuts, and garnished with garam masala and fresh cilantro. Copious amounts of ghee make this extra decadent, so be sure you have a batch of ghee on hand before making this recipe. There are many different styles of biryani, with regional variations throughout India. Ours is a vegetable version, with cashews and raisins. Serve it with dahi, plain yogurt, or raita on the side. Biryani is elaborate, delicately spiced, and rich in flavors—perfect for your next special occasion.

PREP TIME: 20 MINUTES,
PLUS 10 MINUTES SOAKING

COOK TIME: 50 MINUTES

YIELD: SERVES 4 TO 6

BASMATI RICE

1½ cups premium basmati rice

5 bay leaves

4 black cardamom pods

4 black peppercorns

4 cinnamon sticks

4 green cardamom pods

4 star anise

4 whole cloves

3 whole mace pieces

1¼ teaspoons sea salt

2 tablespoons ghee, divided

½ teaspoon saffron, soaked in
2 tablespoons water

Warming Garam Masala (page 45),
to garnish

Fresh cilantro, to garnish

1 | **FOR THE BASMATI RICE:** In a medium bowl, rinse the rice in four to five changes of lukewarm water or until it runs relatively clear. Cover with lukewarm water and soak the rice for 10 minutes.

2 | Rinse the rice again and drain. In a large pot, combine the rice, bay leaves, black cardamom, peppercorns, cinnamon, green cardamom, star anise, cloves, mace, and salt. Fill the pot with plenty of water as if you were cooking pasta, about 3 inches above the rice. On medium-high heat, cook the rice for about 10 minutes or until the rice is al dente, and do not stir. Take care not to overcook the rice. Drain the rice through a strainer and transfer to a large bowl.

3 | Using a thin, flat utensil, gently fold in 1 tablespoon ghee and mix the saffron, with its soaking water, into the rice. Set aside.

(continued)

VEGETABLE LAYER

2 tablespoons ghee

1 cup finely chopped onions

2 cups mixed vegetables (diced cauliflower, diced peeled carrots, peas, finely chopped fresh green beans, corn)

1 teaspoon coriander powder

1 teaspoon cumin powder

½ teaspoon turmeric powder

¼ teaspoon Indian chili powder

½ cup raw jumbo cashews, halved

¼ cup golden raisins

½ teaspoon Warming Garam Masala (page 45)

½ teaspoon sea salt, or to taste

4 | **FOR THE VEGETABLE LAYER:** In a medium non-stick pot or pan on medium-high heat, heat the ghee. Add the onions and fry them for 10 minutes or until translucent and softened. Reduce the heat to medium, then add the mixed vegetables and stir to combine. Sprinkle in the coriander, cumin, turmeric, and chili powder and mix. Add the cashews and raisins. Sprinkle in the garam masala and salt and mix well to combine. Cook for 10 minutes or until the vegetables are cooked and tender. Set aside.

5 | Preheat the oven to 325°F.

6 | Grease the bottom and sides of a medium casserole dish or Dutch oven with the remaining 1 tablespoon ghee. Spread half of the rice on the bottom of the dish, and garnish with garam masala and cilantro to taste. Add the vegetable layer, smoothing it evenly over the rice. Garnish with more garam masala and cilantro to taste. Add the remaining rice on top. Using the handle of a wooden spoon, indent a few holes through the biryani to allow steam to release. Cover with aluminum foil and bake in the center of the oven for 20 to 25 minutes.

7 | Garnish with more garam masala and cilantro to taste. Serve with Basic Cooling Cucumber Raita (page 60) on the side.

NOTE: If you have pistachios on hand, feel free to add in a couple of tablespoons (halve them first), or substitute them altogether for the cashews.

LEMON COCONUT CRANBERRY PULLAO

I originally created this festive rice dish for our Epicurean Indian Valentine's menu. Paired with Mapled Tandoori Salmon with Mint (page 194), it makes a delectable and attractive meal. I also serve this rice over the holidays and at other festive dinners throughout the year. Nestled among fluffy, long basmati rice grains are dried cranberries, which add a slight sweetness and a touch of tartness. The hints of lemon from the lemon peel give a distinctive scent to every bite.

PREP TIME: 10 MINUTES,
PLUS 10 MINUTES SOAKING

COOK TIME: 15 MINUTES

YIELD: SERVES 4

1 cup basmati rice

1 tablespoon ghee

3 green cardamom pods

3 star anise

¼ cup dried desiccated coconut, unsweetened

2 tablespoons dried cranberries

¾ teaspoon sea salt, or to taste

1½ cups water, plus extra if necessary

¼ teaspoon turmeric powder

1 teaspoon lemon zest

2 teaspoons freshly squeezed lemon juice

Warming Garam Masala (page 45), to garnish

Fresh cilantro, finely chopped, to garnish

1 | In a large bowl, rinse the rice in four or five changes of lukewarm water until the water runs relatively clear. Drain and cover with fresh lukewarm water and soak the rice for 10 minutes.

2 | Rinse the rice again in a couple more changes of lukewarm water. Drain.

3 | In a medium non-stick pan or pot on medium-high heat, melt the ghee. Add the cardamom and star anise. Fry for 1 minute or until the cardamom pods swell and the spices are fragrant.

4 | Add the drained rice, coconut, and cranberries and sprinkle in the salt. Using a flat utensil, gently fold so each grain of rice is evenly coated with ghee. Be gentle with the rice at this stage, as the rice grains can break.

5 | Pour in the water, enough to just cover the grains, sprinkle in the turmeric, and gently give it a stir. Cover with a lid and bring to a boil on medium-high heat. Do not stir. Cook the rice until the water is completely absorbed, about 10 minutes. Add the lemon zest and juice, and gently fold into the rice. To check if the rice is fully cooked, take a couple of grains and pinch them between your thumb and index finger. If the rice is still al dente, sprinkle in an extra 2 to 3 tablespoons water and gently mix into the rice.

6 | Remove from the heat and allow the rice to stand for 5 to 10 minutes, covered with a lid. To serve, fluff the rice with a fork and garnish with a sprinkle of garam masala and cilantro to taste.

NOTE: You can transfer this to a large platter to serve it family-style. For a more upscale presentation, press the rice into a well-oiled ramekin and turn it out onto the plate, then garnish it with a sprinkle of garam masala and fresh cilantro.

12

MITHAI, TRADITIONAL INDIAN SWEETS & MODERN INDIAN DESSERTS

Made with ingredients such as green cardamom, rosewater, saffron, pistachios, ghee, and cream, it's no wonder Indian sweets are so decadent and beloved! Indian sweets feature in an Indian meal alongside savory, spicy curries to refresh the palate and provide a harmony of contrasting flavors. On occasions such as a celebratory dinner, an Indian banquet, or a festival season like Diwali, sweets are shared and enjoyed with much pomp and gusto.

I'm not going to lie—I'm quite choosy when it comes to Indian sweets, desserts, and sweetmeats. If they're not prepared with the freshest and purest ingredients and with the utmost care with the right balance of sugar, ghee, and spices, the result can be either oversweet, too rich, or heavy. This is why I most prefer to eat homemade Indian desserts where I can control the quality of ingredients, the type of fat, and the sugar balance. The recipes in this chapter include a variety of our most beloved sweet treats, perfect for all occasions or as an everyday indulgence.

GULAB JAMUNS

Gulab jamuns are Indian milk-based "doughnuts," deep-fried, then immersed *in an ambrosial and heavenly rosewater-scented syrup infused with saffron threads (gulab means "rose"). The syrup itself is divine, but when eaten with the pillowy soaked doughnut, it's like two treats in one! I particularly enjoy gulab jamuns slightly warmed, but they can also be served chilled on a hot day.*

PREP TIME: 50 MINUTES

COOK TIME: 45 MINUTES

YIELD: 32 TO 36 GULAB JAMUNS

2 teaspoons green cardamom seeds

2 cups whole milk powder

¼ cup all-purpose flour

2 tablespoons fine semolina (suji)

¼ teaspoon baking soda

¾ cup Creamy Dahi (page 40) or Balkan-style yogurt, plus extra if necessary

Sunflower oil for deep-frying

Pistachios, finely ground, to garnish

ROSEWATER SYRUP

4 cups water

3 cups raw cane sugar

½ teaspoon saffron

1 teaspoon rosewater

1 | In a heavy mortar and pestle, coarsely grind the cardamom until all the seeds are cracked.

2 | In a large paraat or bowl, combine the milk powder, flour, semolina, cracked cardamom, and baking soda and mix thoroughly. Add the dahi and mix to form a firm dough. The dough will start off sticky but will come together as it combines. If it looks too dry, add more dahi, about 1 tablespoon or more if necessary. If mixing the dough with your hands, remove any excess sticky dough by simply taking a little flour and rubbing your hands together. Set the dough aside for 5 minutes to rest.

3 | **FOR THE ROSEWATER SYRUP:** In a large pot, bring the water to a boil, then add the sugar and stir to dissolve. Bring the mixture back to a boil, then reduce the heat to medium. Simmer for 35 to 40 minutes to reduce to a syrup, making sure the syrup doesn't get too thick. The desired consistency is neither too watery nor too thick. Stir in the saffron and the rosewater. With the lid on, keep the syrup on low heat, as the gulab jamuns should be placed in warm syrup.

4 | Gently knead the gulab jamun dough and then make small, even-sized, smooth round balls, 1 inch in diameter. Be sure that each ball is extremely smooth, with no cracks.

5 | Line a tray or large plate with paper towel for draining the oil.

6 | Fill a kadhai, wok, or deep-fryer with oil 1½ inches deep. Heat the oil on medium. Test the oil temperature by dropping a little dough into the hot oil. If the dough immediately floats to the top, the oil is ready. At this point, start carefully adding the dough balls to the hot oil, deep-frying only a few at a time so as not to crowd them. Fry the balls evenly until they become dark golden brown on all sides, taking care that they don't burn. You can use a fork to turn the balls in the oil. Drain on paper towel and transfer immediately to the warm syrup. Allow the gulab jamuns to soak in the syrup thoroughly before serving. For best results, soak overnight.

7 | Sprinkle with ground pistachios. Gulab jamuns will keep an airtight container in the refrigerator for up to 1 week.

It's preferable to make gulab jamuns 1 or 2 days in advance so the rosewater syrup soaks all the way through and they're moist. They can be slightly warmed before serving.

ROSEWATER NAN KATAI

I simply can't get enough of cardamom. *Come the 2 p.m. tea hour when it's time to make a masala chai, I find myself unapologetically taking a deep inhale from the chai masala tin, seeking a momentarily exotic escape from the everyday. The seduction of the chai masala itself is mostly because of the heavenly cardamom. When I was developing the menu for our spice boutique and masala chai cafe, Arvinda's Spices & Chai, I thought about how I could use cardamom in a masala chai dipping cookie. This Indian-style shortbread, nan katai, is the perfect vehicle. In this recipe I use semolina, which is in my mother's original nan katai recipe and gives the shortbread a distinct texture and bite. I've added an extra layer of flavor with rosewater, making this a tempting, melt-in-your-mouth gem of a cookie to serve with a freshly brewed cup of masala chai.*

PREP TIME: 35 MINUTES,
PLUS 15 MINUTES CHILLING

COOK TIME: 15 MINUTES

YIELD: 25 TO 30 NAN KATAI

½ cup salted butter, room temperature

½ cup icing sugar

¼ teaspoon baking soda

1 cup all-purpose flour

¼ cup fine semolina (suji)

1 teaspoon Perfumy Chai Masala (page 46)

2 tablespoons 2% or whole milk

½ teaspoon rosewater (add up to ¾ teaspoon for bolder flavor)

Dried cranberries, to garnish

1 | Line a baking sheet with parchment paper. Set aside.

2 | In a large mixing bowl, cream the butter with the icing sugar. Add the baking soda and combine. Sift in the flour to remove any lumps, then add the semolina. Mix to combine. Sprinkle in the chai masala, then add the milk and rosewater. Knead the ingredients together to make a cookie dough, taking care not to overmix it.

3 | Chill the dough in the refrigerator for 15 minutes so it firms up before rolling the cookies out.

4 | Preheat the oven to 350°F. Knead the cookie dough and make equal-sized 1-inch balls, then flatten them out into patties. Add a dried cranberry to the top of each nan katai. Bake for 13 to 15 minutes or until the bottoms are golden.

5 | Transfer to a wire cake rack and cool for 10 minutes. Serve with a cup of steaming hot masala chai.

NOTE: For an elegant and beautiful presentation, serve nan katai on a cookie platter sprinkled with dried edible rose petals.

DECADENT SHRIKHAND

Every year on my birthday when I was growing up, my mother would ask me what dessert I wanted for my special day. With clockwork-like predictability, I always asked for the same thing—shrikhand. It wasn't a birthday cake I was after, it was this decadent, sweetened yogurt spiced with cardamom and garnished with green pistachios. To me, even one spoonful of shrikhand feels special and indulgent, as it has an incredible richness and creaminess. I no longer reserve making shrikhand as a once-a-year treat; I now make it for a celebratory meal during the festival season or when serving a vegetarian thali. Our Suji Puris (page 205) are a classic match for this dessert, as the crispy fried flatbread complements the sweetness so well.
A spoonful of shrikhand, then a bite of an Indian vegetable curry (subji), a little rice with dal, then another round of shrikhand, and I'm elated over my most favorite food ever. I hope you enjoy this recipe as much as I do!

PREP TIME: 15 MINUTES,
PLUS OVERNIGHT DRAINING

YIELD: 1½ CUPS

3 cups Balkan-style yogurt

½ cup icing sugar, or to taste

1 teaspoon Perfumy Chai Masala
(page 46)

1 teaspoon saffron

¼ teaspoon rosewater

2 teaspoons coarsely ground
almonds, plus extra to garnish

2 teaspoons finely ground
pistachios, plus extra to garnish

1 | Line a medium strainer or colander with cheesecloth, then place a plate under the strainer. Place the yogurt in the lined strainer to allow excess liquid to drain out. Keep in the refrigerator overnight.

2 | Scoop out the yogurt cheese into a medium bowl. It should be firm, with excess moisture removed.

3 | Sift the icing sugar into the bowl, then stir to combine. Add the chai masala, saffron, and rosewater and mix well. Add more sugar, if desired.

4 | Mix in the almonds and pistachios.

5 | Chill in the refrigerator before serving. Serve with a vegetarian Indian meal or thali with Suji Puris (page 205), and garnish with almonds and pistachios to taste.

NOTE: Although it won't result in exactly the same consistency, you can substitute making your own yogurt cheese with a full-fat Greek-style yogurt for ease and convenience. Serve this as a decadent dessert topped with fresh tropical fruit such as cubed mango, chunked pineapple, or passionfruit, or with local fruit like strawberries or raspberries.

CHOCOLATE ORANGE & VANILLA CARDAMOM BARFI

Back in 1997, *we were invited to participate in Eat to the Beat, a charity gala to raise funds and awareness for Willow Breast & Hereditary Cancer Support. In its first year, chefs were asked to prepare a dessert or sweet. We chose to prepare layered barfi, a milk-based Indian-style fudge traditionally made and shared on festive occasions. I'm taking that same base recipe but giving it a twist—this is a new and special combination I created especially for my brother, Paresh, who is the biggest chocolate lover I know and who also fancies the flavor of orange. I'm adopting this classic pairing of chocolate and orange and applying it to our traditional barfi recipe so it's modern, exquisite, and exceptionally decadent with vanilla, dark chocolate, and a hint of juicy citrus.*

PREP TIME: 1 HOUR, PLUS 4 HOURS TO OVERNIGHT CHILLING

COOK TIME: 1 MINUTE

YIELD: 16 TO 20 PIECES

¼ cup ghee

½ cup icing sugar

1½ cups whole milk powder

¼ cup half-and-half cream

¼ cup almond flour

½ teaspoon green cardamom seeds, finely ground

¾ teaspoon pure vanilla extract

1 tablespoon finely slivered pistachios, to garnish

1 | Line an 8-inch diameter, 1-inch deep stainless-steel plate with parchment paper. Set aside.

2 | In a large non-stick skillet on medium-low heat, melt the ghee. Stir in the icing sugar to combine.

3 | Sift in the milk powder and mix to combine. Add the cream, almond flour, cardamom, and vanilla and stir so all the ingredients become uniform. Remove the barfi from the pan, and once it is cool enough to handle, knead it with your hands so all the mixture comes together.

4 | Press the barfi into the prepared plate and smooth it out into an even layer. You can use the bottom of a small stainless-steel bowl or katori or a spatula to compress the mixture firmly into the plate.

(continued)

CHOCOLATE TOPPING

3½ ounces dark chocolate (70% cocoa), chopped

3½ ounces milk chocolate, chopped

1 tablespoon salted butter

2 tablespoons half-and-half cream

1 teaspoon orange blossom water

5 | FOR THE CHOCOLATE TOPPING: Melt the chocolates using a double boiler (see Note). Once the chocolate is smooth and melted, stir in the butter. Add the cream and orange blossom water and stir to combine. The chocolate topping should be glossy.

6 | Using a spatula, layer the chocolate topping on top of the barfi and smooth it out evenly. Sprinkle on the pistachios to garnish. Refrigerate for at least 4 hours or overnight.

7 | Cut the barfi into 1¼-inch squares or diamond shapes. For a bite-sized barfi, cut the squares into 1-inch pieces. Serve as a decadent treat!

NOTE: Chocolate is often melted in a double boiler so that direct heat—either direct from the stovetop or a microwave—does not come in contact and overcook the chocolate. Set up a double boiler by boiling water in a small saucepan or heavy-bottomed pot over the stove. Nest a slightly larger stainless-steel bowl on top of the saucepan, ensuring it doesn't come into contact with the boiling water. Add the chocolate to the bowl and it will slowly melt from the accumulated steam.

RAS MALAI

Ras Malai are pressed little paneer-like patties called chenna, which are immersed in a bath of reduced milk scented with saffron, crushed green cardamon seeds, and perfumed rosewater to make them heavenly and delicious. This is a celebrated dessert that's said to have originated in Bengal, but it's well loved all over the Indian subcontinent. Ras translates to "juice," and malai means "cream"—this dessert is all about the milk. An important point to note when making ras malai at home: the process of cheese making for this is similar to that of paneer, but the cheese needs to be made fresh right before preparing this recipe, otherwise it becomes too tough and unable to absorb the fragrant milk. Be extra careful not to overcook the cheese, and quickly cool and lower the temperature using ice.

PREP TIME: 1 HOUR,
PLUS OVERNIGHT SOAKING

COOK TIME: 1½ HOURS

YIELD: 10 TO 14 RAS MALAI

CHENNA

8 cups whole milk

¼ cup white vinegar

2 cups ice cubes

½ teaspoon green cardamom seeds, finely ground

FRAGRANT MILK SAUCE (RAS)

2 cups half-and-half cream

1 cup whole milk

½ cup raw cane sugar, or more to taste

1 teaspoon green cardamom seeds, crushed

½ teaspoon saffron

¼ teaspoon rosewater

1 | FOR THE CHENNA: Line a medium colander or strainer with cheesecloth and place it in the sink. In a medium pot on medium-high heat, bring the milk to a boil, stirring to ensure it doesn't burn. Once the milk starts to form a lot of bubbles on the surface, quickly remove the pot from the heat, then add the vinegar to curdle the milk. Once curdled, add the ice cubes to stop the cooking process. If the liquid is still very hot, take caution and wear gloves for this next step. Strain the chenna into the cheesecloth, gently squeeze to remove any excess liquid, and then let it sit in the colander in the sink for 45 minutes to allow the liquid to drain out.

2 | FOR THE FRAGRANT MILK SAUCE (RAS): In a medium pot on medium-low heat, heat the cream, milk, and sugar and stir to combine. Simmer for 45 minutes or until the milk slightly thickens, stirring occasionally. Add the cardamom, saffron, and rosewater, stir, and simmer for another 5 minutes. Remove from the heat and cool to room temperature, then refrigerate to chill.

(continued)

SUGAR SYRUP WATER

3 cups water

⅔ cup raw cane sugar

GARNISH

1½ tablespoons finely sliced almonds

1½ tablespoons finely chopped pistachios

3 | FOR THE SUGAR SYRUP WATER: In a separate medium pot, combine the water and sugar and stir to dissolve as you bring the mixture to a boil. Reduce the heat to medium-low and continue to simmer for 20 to 25 minutes. The syrup should have a watery consistency, not thick.

4 | Meanwhile, in a medium bowl, mix the chenna with the finely ground cardamom seeds. Knead well so the chenna comes together with a smooth consistency. Make 10 to 14 small ras malai balls, making sure they are smooth. Using your palms, flatten them into patties. Gently place the patties in the sugar syrup water and simmer on medium heat for 15 minutes or until the patties are cooked and become spongy and soft. The patties will expand in size.

5 | With a slotted spoon, remove the patties from the sugar syrup water, gently squeeze them to remove any excess water, and add them to the Fragrant Milk Sauce. Refrigerate overnight to allow the ras malai milk to penetrate fully into the patties.

6 | Serve ras malai in a small bowl garnished with almonds and pistachios.

NOTE: The fragrant ras malai milk is so delicious and versatile—drench your favorite cubed fruit like mangoes, apples, peaches, red grapes, or pineapples with this milk and serve it chilled in a bowl. This is perfect in summer!

CARAMELIZED CHAI-SPICED BANANAS

In fresh produce markets in India, *baby bananas are everywhere. Either red or a warm golden yellow (they are different varieties), they are peppered with dark spots because they quickly ripen in heat and are specially merchandized right at the front of market stalls to seduce you with their strong banana aroma. Some baby bananas are sweeter than their bigger counterparts, but for this recipe I've used the larger variety as the baby ones are not readily available. The jaggery that we use to caramelize the bananas can be sourced from South Asian grocery stores. Serve these caramelized bananas with a dollop of creamy Decadent Shrikhand (page 234) on the side or a scoop of vanilla ice cream, if desired.*

PREP TIME: 10 MINUTES

COOK TIME: 10 MINUTES

YIELD: SERVES 4

4 ripe bananas, peeled

2 tablespoons raw cashew halves, to garnish

1 tablespoon ghee or salted butter

¼ cup jaggery or brown or maple sugar (see note)

⅓ cup half-and-half cream

1 teaspoon Perfumy Chai Masala (page 46)

½ teaspoon ginger powder

2 tablespoons blueberries, to garnish

2 tablespoons coconut chips or dried desiccated coconut, unsweetened

2 tablespoons coarsely chopped dark chocolate, to garnish

4 fresh mint leaves, to garnish

1 | Cut the peeled bananas in half and slice lengthwise. Set aside.

2 | Heat a large non-stick skillet on medium heat. Add the cashews and gently toast for a couple of minutes or until fragrant. Transfer to a small bowl and set aside as a garnish.

3 | In the same large non-stick skillet on medium heat, melt the ghee. Add the jaggery and stir to combine. Stir in the cream and sprinkle in the chai masala and ginger powder. Mix together to create a sauce.

4 | Gently add the bananas, coating with the ghee and jaggery mixture, and cook for 3 to 5 minutes or until soft.

5 | Serve the caramelized bananas as a plated dessert garnished with the toasted cashews, blueberries, coconut chips, dark chocolate, and a mint leaf.

NOTE: If using brown or maple sugar instead of jaggery, consider reducing the amount slightly, as the results may be a touch sweeter.

ALMOND, COCONUT & CRANBERRY SNOWBALL LADOOS

I created this recipe many years ago as a way of making healthier ladoos, one of the most loved Indian sweets that are usually round in shape and consumed regularly during festive times of year. My version has a similar flavor, texture, and richness of the traditional ladoo, but with lighter ingredients (traditional ladoos are heavy on fat and sugar). At the time I created these, I was running in half-marathons and found these power-packed balls gave me a much-needed energy boost. Then, our friend and culinary colleague, Mary Luz, helped us with a brilliant cooking workshop called the Merry Masala Cookie Exchange where we featured Indian spice–infused treats for the holiday season. This recipe was a part of the delicious event. The ladoos are perfect for the holidays as they look incredibly festive and are reminiscent of snowballs.

PREP TIME: 35 MINUTES,
PLUS 15 MINUTES CHILLING

YIELD: 24 TO 28 LADOOS

1 cup crunchy almond butter

1 cup dried desiccated coconut, unsweetened, plus extra for coating

½ cup almond flour

½ cup dried cranberries

¼ cup raisins

¼ cup raw sesame seeds

¼ cup honey

1 tablespoon Perfumy Chai Masala (page 46)

1 | In a medium bowl, place all the ingredients. Mix well to combine thoroughly. Chill the mixture in the refrigerator for 15 minutes so it becomes firm.

2 | Take 1 tablespoon of mixture and form it into a ball. Continue with the remaining mixture.

3 | Place ¾ cup coconut in a shallow dish, or use as much as required for coating the ladoos. Coat the ladoos in the coconut, shaking off any excess. Ladoos will keep in an airtight container in the refrigerator for up to 3 weeks.

NOTE: If the oil in the almond butter has separated, be sure to stir well to reincorporate it before making this recipe. If the almond butter has slightly hardened or solidified, gently heat it to make the ladoos easier to roll out.

GARAM MASALA GINGERBREAD CAKE WITH CLEMENTINE TOFFEE SAUCE

I've been baking with garam masala for years, as it adds distinctive Indian flavors to baked treats. Garam masala especially complements any dessert containing dark chocolate, fruit, or rum, and in this recipe, it's absolutely perfect. Serve this decadent cake over the holiday season—one drizzle of the festive clementine toffee sauce takes this dessert over the top.

PREP TIME: 40 MINUTES, PLUS 10 MINUTES COOLING

COOK TIME: 55 MINUTES

YIELD: 10-CUP BUNDT CAKE

½ cup salted butter, softened

¾ cup jaggery or brown sugar

2 eggs

1 teaspoon pure vanilla extract

1½ cups all-purpose flour, sifted

3 tablespoons Warming Garam Masala (page 45)

2 tablespoons cocoa powder

1 teaspoon baking powder

1 teaspoon baking soda

¾ cup mixed citrus peel

¼ cup raisins (see Note)

¾ cup 2% or whole milk

¼ cup Creamy Dahi (page 40) or Balkan-style yogurt

Icing sugar, to garnish

8 fresh mint leaves, to garnish

CLEMENTINE TOFFEE SAUCE

¼ cup salted butter

½ cup jaggery or brown sugar

¼ cup half-and-half cream

1 tablespoon fresh clementine or orange juice

1 teaspoon clementine or orange zest

1 teaspoon pure vanilla extract

1 | Using a pastry brush and oil, grease a 10-cup Bundt pan well, taking care to get the oil into every crease in the Bundt pan. Preheat the oven to 325°F.

2 | In a large bowl, cream the butter with the jaggery. Beat in the eggs and stir in the vanilla. Fold in the flour, garam masala, cocoa, baking powder, and baking soda. Add the mixed peel and raisins. Mix to combine well.

3 | In a small bowl, whisk together the milk and yogurt and fold it into the batter.

4 | Pour the batter into the Bundt pan and bake in the center of the oven for 50 to 55 minutes.

5 | FOR THE CLEMENTINE TOFFEE SAUCE: In a small non-stick, heavy-bottomed saucepan on medium heat, melt the butter. Add the jaggery and stir in the cream. Simmer for 10 minutes or just until the toffee sauce has thickened up. Mix in the clementine juice, clementine zest, and vanilla. Stir to combine and simmer for 5 minutes.

6 | Remove the cake from the oven and insert a knife into the center to test its doneness. If the knife comes out clean, the cake is fully cooked. Allow the cake to cool for 10 minutes. Using a small knife, cut along the edges of the Bundt pan to loosen the cake from the pan. Be sure to cut around the center hole as well. Insert the knife deep down the sides of the pan, which will ensure the cake will come out easily. Turn the cake out onto a wire cake rack to remove it from the Bundt pan, then fully cool it before serving.

7 | Serve a slice of cake with a drizzle of the clementine toffee sauce on top. Garnish with a dusting of icing sugar to taste and a mint leaf.

NOTE: If you feel inclined to do so, soak the raisins in 3 tablespoons dark rum for 1 hour before adding them to the cake batter for another layer of festive flavor!

WARM SUJI HALWA

This is another popular Indian sweet—a semolina pudding with saffron, raisins, and nuts. Suji halwa is the most common Indian sweet prepared as prasad, an auspicious offering to deities. Once it's been served as an offering, only then is it consumed as a divine blessing. Semolina is commonly found in South Asian grocery stores as well as in larger grocery retailers, either in the rice and grains aisle or in the baking section. If you can only find fine semolina, you can certainly use it, but it will yield a creamy, buttery texture as opposed to the grainy, thick texture of coarse semolina. If given a choice, go for the coarse.

PREP TIME: 5 MINUTES

COOK TIME: 20 MINUTES

YIELD: SERVES 4

¼ teaspoon saffron

1 tablespoon warm water

2 tablespoons ghee

½ cup coarse semolina (suji)

1 cup 2% or whole milk

¼ cup raw cane sugar

1 tablespoon raisins

1 teaspoon Perfumy Chai Masala (page 46)

Slivered almonds, to garnish

1 | In a small bowl, soak the saffron in the warm water. Set aside.

2 | In a small non-stick, heavy-bottomed pot on medium heat, melt the ghee. Add the semolina and toast for 7 to 10 minutes, stirring continuously, until the semolina turns golden brown and has a toasted fragrance.

3 | Add the milk and stir. Cover and cook on low heat until all the moisture is absorbed (this takes only a couple of minutes).

4 | Add the sugar, raisins, and chai masala, then add the saffron with its soaking water. Mix and cook further for a few more minutes.

5 | Transfer to a serving dish and garnish with almonds to taste. Serve warm with a full Indian meal.

EXOTIC INDIAN-STYLE FRUIT SALAD

Mangoes, which are native to India, are known as the empress of fruits. It's said that with the first bite of a mango comes immense happiness, prosperity, knowledge, and joy. We like to take it one step further with our Indian fruit salad. It's a fruit lover's dream, jeweled with pomegranate seeds, red grapes, pineapple chunks, and fresh mint, which slips through the sweetness of the luscious fruits. With yet another layer of flavor, I laced in a tart lime juice dressing nuanced with chaat masala, imparting hints of sour, chili, and black pepper. This is a special recipe to highlight the flavors of this enticing spice blend.

PREP TIME: 20 MINUTES

YIELD: 4 CUPS

1 tablespoon freshly squeezed lime juice

1 teaspoon Tangy Chaat Masala (page 48)

1 Alphonso or Ataulfo mango, peeled

1 pomegranate, seeded (about 1 cup seeds)

1 cup red grapes, halved

1 cup cubed pineapple

2 tablespoons finely chopped fresh mint leaves

1 | In a small bowl, mix the lime juice and chaat masala together. Set aside.

2 | Cut the mango into 1-inch cubes.

3 | In a medium bowl, mix together the mangoes, pomegranate seeds, red grapes, pineapple cubes, and mint. Sprinkle on the lime juice and chaat masala mixture and mix again. Serve this fruit salad in dessert cups or coupe glasses.

NOTE: For this recipe, choose a non-fibrous variety of mango—Alphonso is the ideal choice, although Ataulfo mangoes are also an excellent choice! Be sure to select a ripe but firm mango so you can easily cut it into cubes. When peeling the mango, try not to bruise the flesh.

MASALA COFFEE

It was surprising for me to learn that in a nation of predominantly tea drinkers, coffee chains and cafés have become so popular in India. On one trip to Mumbai, my family friend who was my city guide for the day passed on the idea of going for a masala chai and recommended coffee instead. This recipe is inspired by a cappuccino I had at a ritzy café in Mumbai, but it was really created for our masala chai café especially for coffee lovers. After much trial and error and rounds of sampling with staff and customers, I discovered the right balance for a beautifully subtle spiced coffee made with a single-estate, fair-trade organic beans, hot milk, cardamom, and a slight note of sweetness to bring out the flavors. Customers just loved it, and I think you will too.

PREP TIME: 1 MINUTE

COOK TIME: 5 MINUTES

YIELD: 1 CUP

1 teaspoon Perfumy Chai Masala (page 46)

3 tablespoons finely ground dark roast coffee

⅔ cup boiling water

⅓ cup whole milk

1 teaspoon raw cane sugar (optional)

1 | Line a single-cup pour-over coffee cone with a paper filter and place it over a glass measuring cup. Sprinkle the chai masala at the bottom of the cone, then top it with coffee. Pour in the boiling water and allow for the coffee to percolate through the filter into the measuring cup.

2 | In a small non-stick saucepan on medium-high heat, heat the milk. Just as bubbles start to form, add the sugar and stir to dissolve.

3 | Add the brewed coffee to the saucepan stirring to combine it with the milk. Allow it to come to a boil. Remove it from the heat and pour the masala coffee into a mug. Serve hot and enjoy!

NOTE: If you don't have a single-cup pour-over coffee cone, you can follow the same method using a standard percolator coffee machine and adjust the chai masala and the ground coffee quantities depending on how many cups you wish to brew. Choose a high-quality, fair-trade organic coffee for best results.

KESAR BADAM DOODH

One step forward, two steps back. *If you're having that kind of day, consider having this soothing beverage of saffron-scented chai-spiced milk with almonds to help you get back on track. In my mother's school-aged years when she was preparing for exams, her grandfather would suggest this drink to help her stay focused and gain mental clarity. An avid practitioner of Ayurveda, my great-grandfather generously shared his Ayurvedic wisdom and recipes like this one in every way he could. Naturally, my mother did as her grandfather had done while my brother and I were going through exams, so we also became accustomed to drinking this restorative beverage in our adolescence.*

PREP TIME: 10 MINUTES,
PLUS 1 HOUR SOAKING

COOK TIME: 10 MINUTES

YIELD: 2 CUPS

2 tablespoons whole almonds

2 cups 2% or whole milk

1½ teaspoons Perfumy Chai Masala (page 46)

2½ teaspoons jaggery or raw cane sugar (optional)

Pinch of saffron

½ teaspoon finely ground pistachios, to garnish

1 | In a small bowl, soak the almonds in warm water for 1 hour.

2 | Remove the skins from the almonds. Place the almonds in a small food processor or a clean coffee grinder and finely grind.

3 | In a medium non-stick saucepan on medium-high heat, bring the milk to a gentle simmer, then add the chai masala, jaggery, and saffron. Continue to simmer for a couple of minutes to allow the jaggery to dissolve.

4 | Add the almonds and continue to simmer for a few more minutes to allow the saffron to release its flavor.

5 | Pour into four small demitasse cups or two mugs. Garnish with pistachios.

NOTE: You can sweeten this hot beverage with honey, but I recommend stirring in the honey after pouring the beverage into mugs, rather than simmering the honey in the pot.

PINEAPPLE JAL JEERA

On our travels throughout India, *a common welcome drink we enjoyed when arriving at a new destination or visiting homes was jal jeera, a water and lime beverage infused with cumin and other spices, such as black peppercorns, red chilies, black salt, and amchoor, that energizes the senses. This drink can be quite sour and spicy, offering both hydration and aiding with digestion, but my mom's version combines pineapple juice to balance out the sourness with a tropical sweetness that harmoniously mixes well with the multilayered spices. She often serves it at the end of a cooking class with the meal, as it's the perfect thirst-quenching drink after a long day in a hot kitchen.*

PREP TIME: 10 MINUTES

COOK TIME: 5 MINUTES

YIELD: 4 CUPS

½ teaspoon cumin seeds

3 cups pure pineapple juice

1 cup cold filtered water

Juice of 1 lime

¾ to 1 teaspoon Tangy Chaat Masala (page 48)

½ teaspoon concentrated tamarind paste

4 fresh mint leaves, to garnish (optional)

1 | Heat a small skillet on medium-high heat and add the cumin seeds. Using a wooden spoon, gently stir the spices until they become slightly golden brown and fragrant. You can also pick up the skillet to gently toss the spices until they become toasted. This may take a couple of minutes, but the real indicator is when the cumin seeds are light golden.

2 | Transfer the cumin seeds to a mortar and pestle. When cool, grind into a fine powder.

3 | In a medium pitcher, combine the pineapple juice, water, and cumin. Add the lime juice, chaat masala, and tamarind. Whisk all the ingredients together so the tamarind dissolves into the juice.

4 | Chill in the refrigerator and serve cold. Strain the juice before serving in glasses garnished with a mint leaf.

NOTE: Straining the juice will make it smoother so the fine spice powders don't irritate the throat, but if you prefer the jal jeera to be more intense and spicy, you can skip the straining step.

SPARKLING LIMBU PANI

On the western coast of India lies Varkala Beach. With rocky cliffs and sandy beaches, the area is frequented by surfers and backpackers and is a place where time seems to stop. On a memorable visit there, my mother and I descended from our hilltop house to a path dotted with shops, eateries, and a refreshment stand, where we ordered limbu pani, an Indian-style lemonade. It's a commonly found beverage across India, and you can have it either sweet or salty. The salty version replenishes lost electrolytes, and the sweet one is a welcome thirst quencher. Our recipe is inspired by this drink, but we've added spices, namely chaat masala, to add an extra layer of sourness from the amchoor and a dash of heat from red chilies.

PREP TIME: 10 MINUTES, PLUS 15 MINUTES CHILLING

COOK TIME: 10 MINUTES

YIELD: 4 CUPS

3 to 4 lemons

½ teaspoon Tangy Chaat Masala (page 48)

½ cup ice cubes

12 raspberries or blackberries

8 fresh mint leaves, finely chopped (optional)

3 cups sparkling water

4 strips lemon peel, to garnish

SIMPLE SYRUP

½ cup raw cane sugar

½ cup water

1 tablespoon lemon zest

1 | Extract the juice from the lemons, yielding about ¾ cup of fresh lemon juice. Whisk the chaat masala into the juice until it is well incorporated.

2 | **FOR THE SIMPLE SYRUP:** In a small non-stick saucepan on medium-high heat, combine the sugar, water, and lemon zest. Bring to a simmer for 7 to 9 minutes or until the sugar dissolves. Transfer to a glass measuring cup or bowl and allow it to cool down.

3 | Combine the fresh lemon juice mixture with the simple syrup and chill it in the refrigerator for at least 15 minutes.

4 | Place a few ice cubes in each of four glasses. Divide the raspberries equally between the glasses, then pour a quarter of the lemon juice–simple syrup mixture into each one. Add a bit of mint to each glass.

5 | Carefully top each glass with sparkling water. Garnish with a lemon peel and serve immediately.

NOTE: Make the lemon juice–simple syrup mixture ahead of time and chill it in the refrigerator. Top the drinks with sparkling water right before serving

PEACHY SWEET MANGO LASSI

Salted or sweet, lassi is a delicious Indian-style smoothie that is perfect for a hot summer day. On its own, lassi is quite filling, as it's high in protein from the milk and yogurt and chock-full of juicy, ripe mangoes. In Ayurveda, when mango combines with dairy it's considered a whole meal. My great-grandfather often had this in lieu of a full dinner, so consider lassi to be a healthy snack, a mini meal, or a smoothie treat.

PREP TIME: 25 MINUTES

YIELD: ABOUT 4 CUPS

1 cup half-and-half cream

½ teaspoon saffron

2 ripe Alphonso mangoes, peeled

1 medium ripe peach, peeled

¾ cup Creamy Dahi (page 40) or Balkan-style yogurt

2 tablespoons raw cane sugar, or extra to taste

1 teaspoon Perfumy Chai Masala (page 46)

2 cups ice cubes

4 fresh mint leaves, to garnish

1 | In a glass measuring cup or small bowl, combine the cream and the saffron. Stir and allow it to sit for 10 minutes.

2 | Finely cube the mangoes and the peach.

3 | In a blender, place the mangoes, peaches, dahi, sugar, and chai masala. Blend until the fruit is puréed and the mixture is smooth.

4 | Add the ice cubes and saffron-infused cream and blend again until the lassi is uniform and smooth. Lassi consistency should be thick like a smoothie, but if it's too thick, thin it out with a little water.

5 | Pour the lassi into four glasses of your choice and serve each with a straw and a mint leaf garnish.

NOTE: Ataulfo mangoes are a delicious substitute for Alphonso.

FESTIVE & SEASONAL INDIAN MENUS

Some things in life are better together! In Indian cuisine and tradition, certain dishes pair together to make a more enjoyable Indian eating experience, and for this reason, we offer our suggestions for meal pairings and special-occasion menus to bring out the best flavors in every recipe. Many of these menus are based on our themed Indian cooking classes.

Plan a get-together around one of the menus or choose a special holiday on which you can treat loved ones to an Indian dinner. In Arvinda's words, treating someone you love to a home-cooked meal is the best gift you can give!

Don't feel as if you need to make all the items in each menu, as these are meant as general guidelines for creating a menu. A typical Indian meal consists of a flatbread, vegetable, dal, main curry, and rice, with pickles, raita, chutneys, and desserts on the side. A well-rounded Indian meal should contain four to five items.

A RAJAH'S FEAST

Onion Kale Bhajias, page 99

Mango Peach Chutney, page 62

Shahi Paneer with Shredded Ginger, page 159

Dal Makhani, page 131

Baingan Bharta, page 141

Lamb Korma, page 184

Vegetable Biryani with Saffron & Nuts, page 223

Basic Indian Salad & Condiments, page 65

Whole Wheat Garlic Sesame Naan, page 206

Gulab Jamuns, page 230

Ginger-Spiced Masala Chai, page 254

SOUTH INDIA COCONUTS & CURRY LEAVES

South Indian Fresh Coconut Chutney, page 57

Traditional Keralan Avial, page 145

Kerala-Style Coconut Thoran, page 149

Fragrant South Indian Coconut Shrimp with Curry Leaves, page 177

South Indian Uttapams with Red Onion, Green Chili & Cilantro, page 218

Basic Boiled Fluffy Rice, page 214

Caramelized Chai-Spiced Bananas, page 243

Pineapple Jal Jeera, page 261

BACKYARD TANDOORI BARBECUE

Savory Chaat Papri, page 91

Minty Green Cilantro Chutney, page 53

Sweet & Tangy Tamarind Date Chutney, page 54

Aloo Panch Phoran, page 138

Gujarati-Style Sambharo, page 142

Basic Cooling Cucumber Raita, page 60

Succulent Tandoori Chicken, page 180

Indian-Style Kebabs with Grilling Vegetables, page 187

Whole Wheat Garlic Sesame Naan, page 206

Ras Malai, page 239

Peachy Sweet Mango Lassi, page 265

A BOLLYWOOD BIRTHDAY

Tandoori-Spiced Fish Pakoras, page 105

Hot Chili Tomato Chutney, page 55

Murgh Makhani, page 169

Kashmiri Dum Aloo, page 137

Whole Wheat Garlic Sesame Naan, page 206

Mattar Pullao, page 217

Chocolate Orange & Vanilla Cardamom Barfi, page 237

Sparkling Limbu Pani, page 262

FESTIVAL OF LIGHTS VEGETARIAN THALI

Matchstick Carrot & Green Chilies Achar, page 59

Onion Kale Bhajias, page 99

Mango Peach Chutney, page 62

Tarka Dal Medley, page 128

Kale & Black-Eyed Peas, page 108

Cauliflower & Mixed Vegetables with Crispy Okra, page 150

Eggplant Ravaiya, page 146

Suji Puris, page 205

Mattar Pullao, page 217

Cumin-Scented Papads, page 211

Basic Indian Salad & Condiments, page 65

Decadent Shrikhand, page 234

Warm Suji Halwa, page 249

Kesar Badam Doodh, page 258

DRIED LENTILS & BEANS SOAKING GUIDE

In order for dried lentils and beans to cook well all the way through, they must be soaked first. Soaking times will vary depending on the size and texture of the lentils and beans. Here are general soaking times for the various lentils and beans used in this cookbook:

TYPE OF BEAN/LENTIL	SOAKING TIME
Black-eyed peas	Overnight
Channa dal	2 Hours for stovetop cooking, otherwise 10–15 minutes in Instant Pot
Moong dal spilt	1 Hour
Moong dal split and hulled	30 Minutes
Toor dal	2 Hours
Whole channa (chickpeas)	Overnight
Whole masoor	3 Hours
Whole rajma (red kidney beans)	Overnight
Whole urad	Overnight

LIST OF COMMONLY USED INDIAN WORDS

achar | pickle

adu | ginger

agni | fire, but in the Ayurvedic context it means digestive fires

aloo | potato

anda | egg

Ayurveda | a Sanskrit word meaning the science of life; India's ancient natural system of medicine

belan | a thin rolling pin, tapered at the ends to roll out flatbreads

besan | chickpea flour, also known as gram flour

bhaji | sometimes referred to as *bhajia*, these are deep-fried chopped vegetable fritters in a chickpea flour batter with spices; also refers to a vegetable dish including spinach or greens (cooked or uncooked)

bhurji | scrambled

chaatna | to lick

chaunk | the Hindi word for tempering of spices

chawal | rice

chulha | a traditional clay cooking stove

dabba | a stainless-steel box or container

dahi | homemade Indian yogurt

dhabba | an Indian roadside restaurant or canteen

dhanyavad | the Hindi term for thank you

dosa | South Indian thin rice crepe

garam | warming or hot

idli | South Indian steamed rice cakes

jal | water

jamjo | the Gujarati word for eat; a gesture to tell guests to eat well, take second helpings and enjoy the meal

jeera | cumin

kadhai | a stainless-steel Indian–style wok

kala namak | black salt

kesar | saffron

lasan | garlic

lauki | also referred to as *doodhi*, this is a pale green squash with an airy interior also known as bottle gourd due to its shape. This squash is most often paired with channa dal.

makhan/makhani | butter

masala | a mixture of spices

methi | fenugreek leaves

mithai | an Indian sweet

murgh | chicken

murraba/murrabo | savory, North Indian–style spiced preserve

namak | salt

panch | five

papri | deep-fried crispy flatbreads

paraat | an Indian stainless-steel dish with edges for kneading dough

pav | bread, buns

phodni | the Marathi word for tempering of spices

phoran | the Bengali word for tempering of spices

poriyal | the Tamil word for a stir-fry vegetable preparation

prasad | an auspicious offering to gods and deities

rai | mustard seeds

sabjee/sabji/subji | a term to define a vegetable dish, curry, or preparation

sadhya | a traditional Kerela feast served on a banana leaf

shukriya | a common word in India for thank you

tandoor | a cylindrical clay oven heated with hot coals to cook naan or tandoori chicken. The temperature in a tandoor is ferociously hot, often reaching up to 900°F.

tarka | the Punjabi word for tempering of spices

tawa | a slightly concaved griddle or pan, primarily used for cooking Indian flatbreads; sizes and material can vary from small to large and from cast iron to stainless steel or coated non-stick

thali | a larger stainless-steel plate designed to hold smaller stainless-steel bowls for the purpose of serving a full Indian meal

thoran | a dry vegetable preparation with coconut from Kerela

vaghaar | the Gujarati word for tempering of spices

ACKNOWLEDGEMENTS

Namaste! On behalf of my family we want to express our deepest gratitude to those who have supported us since the start of our culinary adventure.

Many talented people were a part of the creative process of making *New Indian Basics*. First off, a sincere and heartfelt thank-you must go to Robert McCullough for entrusting us to write this cookbook to share our family's story and tradition of Indian cooking with others. Thank you for believing in us, for your warmth and support, your creativity, and brilliant vision of *New Indian Basics* right from the beginning. It's been an absolute delight to finally work with you and from the bottom of my heart, thank you for making my dreams of writing an Indian cookbook come true. Also thank you to our amazing editor, Zoe Maslow, who has been with us on our cookbook writing journey—thank you for your resourcefulness, attention-to-detail, and valuable guidance—we couldn't have made it to the finish line without you. We appreciate all your hard work and your words of encouragement, excitement and passion for *New Indian Basics*! Thank you to Kristin Cochrane, and to Andrew Roberts, Susan Burns, Carla Kean, Colin Rier, and Lana Okerlund; and to Reena, Sandy, Sage and Hayley for making this cookbook so special! Many thanks to our tasters as well.

We thank our family members for lending us words of wisdom that have not been forgotten; this book is a homage to our elders for the Ayurvedic knowledge and cooking traditions that have reached us. Thank you to our cooking mentors for inspiration; and to our family friends, travel companions, distant relatives and culinary colleagues who helped us many years ago—your generosity, acts of kindness and hospitality are always remembered.

Our customers and cooking class students are some of the loveliest people we've met and we'd like to thank them for their support going back as far as 1993. Every time we hear about your Indian cooking excursions, feedback and delicious meals, we're inspired to continue what we do. Without you, we wouldn't be here and your passion for Indian cooking and spices always drives us. Thank you to our retail partners who believe in Arvinda's and have supported us for so many years.

This book would not have been made possible without the incredible collaboration with my family, whom I love very much. To my multi-talented brother Paresh—thank you for your tireless energy on this cookbook and for always standing by me. To my father—the person we see so much drive, work ethic, and energy in. You always said "If you're ever going to do something, you should do it right," and those words stuck. Thank you for so much. To my mother, Arvinda, who has cooked (almost!) every single day of her life, who wishes to inspire others to make Indian cooking easy, fun, and delicious—thank you for your passion and for inspiring us and so many others. My mom really does show her love and caring toward others through food and believes the greatest gift you can give, is cooking with love. Thank you for your mantras and for inspiring all that we do.

And to JJ, you are amazing and I thank you for a lot.

Shukriya, merci, gracias, om shanti! We send those who have crossed our paths blessings of peace and good wishes and thank you for sharing our cooking experience with us. You're in our hearts and our memories. Dhanyavad!

ARVINDA'S INDIAN COOKING ETHOS & MANTRAS FOR LIFE

- Always put good energy, warm wishes, and positive vibrations into your cooking. It will transform your food, and your loved ones will feel this transfer of energy, bringing about feelings of joy and happiness, and good health!

- You are what you eat! Investing the time now in cooking nourishing meals for you and your loved ones will have a ripple effect and will improve overall health and strengthen your relationships in the long term.

- Have gratitude toward Mother Nature for the sun, water, and soil, blessing us with food. Acknowledge the farmers who work so hard to produce the food for our tables.

- Involve family members, loved ones, and children in the cooking process. It is time well spent connecting with each other, learning new recipes, and rewarding each other with a delicious meal made and enjoyed together as a family.

- Get inspired to create something new. Look for ways in your day to inspire a meal. It could be from something you read, a person you had a conversation with, an ingredient in your refrigerator, or something from the pantry.

- Your guests are like gold. Treat them like royalty—a true trademark of Indian hospitality.

- If possible, grow vegetables in your garden. In my first year in Canada, in the early 1970s, I started a garden of Indian herbs and potted tomatoes on my balcony and then rented a larger plot at a community garden to grow my own food, namely Indian varieties of vegetables. My husband now looks after the backyard garden and I look forward to seasonal favorites every year. We are always happy about and grateful for the fruits of our labor and the bounty of produce to pick from to create a delicious meal.

- Use seasonal and local produce where possible and support local farmers. Your food will be delicious and astounding.

- Make your kitchen the most sacred and inviting place in your home. Adorn it with fresh flowers, play some soft music, and make it a warm and cozy space so you will be inclined to spend more time there enjoying the act of cooking.

- Decorate your kitchen with memorabilia from your travels or happy moments in life to inspire you to cook food that reminds you of those people, places, and times.

- Disconnect from electronic devices so you can be present in every step of the cooking process. Connect with nature while cooking by keeping your garden in view as inspiration, if possible. Otherwise, keep potted herbs indoors to create the feeling of nature and connectedness to the earth.

- The greatest gift you can give is cooking with love.

Arvinda

Arvinda

INDEX